CW00927257

REVIEWS FOR COMMERCIAL GOV

David's skill and where he adds huge value is in the way he can apply theoretical frameworks to commercialisation and practically apply them in a tangible way that captures people's imagination around the art of the possible. This book outlines the approach David took with us which was a key factor in helping to take forward our commercialisation agenda so that we can continue to invest in local services for the benefit of local people - *Darren Knight, Executive Director of People and Change, Cheltenham Borough Council*

I would like to endorse and recommend the value of this easy to read book on Commercialisation, it really gives you a straight forward guide to all the issues that Councils need to support them through the commercialisation journey and makes you and your teams think quite differently. The book is full of experience that David brings and case studies to show real practical advice. This new edition adds to the previous edition and expands and builds on the information as life moves on and Councils embrace change - *Tracey Kerly, Chief Executive, Ashford Borough Council*

Most public sector leaders struggle to get the commercial performance that they need. This very timely, revised edition of Commercial Gov is the practical guide that they've been waiting for. - *Elvin Turner, author, "Be Less Zombie: How great companies create dynamic innovation, fearless leadership and passionate people" (Wiley, 2020)*

With this second iteration, David has evolved the tool kit to become an indispensable prerequisite to any organisation, a*nd I would go as far as to say not just limited to public sector,* striving to develop their commercial ambition. By having personal real world experience of the principles and methodologies outlined in this book, I can without hesitation recommend it as essential reading - *Sanjay Mistry – Commercial Programme Manager Cheltenham Borough Council*

The pandemic has caused governments to face historic challenges in delivering affordable and efficient services to citizens who urgently need results. This perfectly timed edition provides the essential frameworks and insights to reaffirm and realign best approaches for success in the years to come - *Chris Bravacos, Chief Executive, The Bravo Group*

The publication of David Elverson's 2nd edition of Commercial Gov, could hardly have come at a more opportune time as local authorities across the UK seek to help their local communities to recover and rebuild following the effects of the global pandemic and associated economic recession. Local government is faced with a perfect storm of diminishing resources and increasing need. Many local authorities are responding to these challenges by seeking to act more commercially. But what does that mean in practice? David's excellent book is packed full of first-hand experience and hard, practical knowledge and is written in an engaging and easy-to-read style. This makes 'Commercial Gov' the 'must have' route map for anyone embarking on a commercialisation journey in local government - *Rob Hann, Head of Local Government, Sharpe Pritchard*

In my review of the first edition of this book I wrote that I would recommend this book both for those beginning to apply commercial thinking within their organisation and for those who have more experience in developing commercialism across the sector. David builds on this foundation in the second edition making it relevant to the new and emerging commercial landscape and providing new insights and tools for commercial managers and leaders at any stage of development – *Ken Lyon, Assistant Chief Executive, South Kesteven District Council*

If you want to know what's happening with commercial development in the public sector, this book is a definitive account of all things "commercial". From strategic positioning, competition, and investments through to implementation of culture, it is a blueprint for taking your organisation through the steps to becoming that entrepreneurial entity.

It controversially highlights a 'creative approach to overhead apportionment' which certainly resonates with my own thought process and I was personally pleased to get to the last chapter on Covid recovery – almost felt like an endorsement that I was thinking and doing all the rights things. *- Paul Jones, Executive Director Finance and Assets, Cheltenham Borough Council. 2019 MJ Award winner for Best Commercial Council and 2019 APSE Award winner for Best Commercialisation & Entrepreneurship Initiative*

COMMERCIAL GOV

a practical guide to commercial development in the public sector

2nd Edition

www.commercialgov.co.uk

COMMERCIAL GOV

COMMERCIAL GOV

a practical guide to commercial development in the public sector

2nd Edition

www.commercialgov.co.uk

DAVID ELVERSON

Commercial Gov - a practical guide to commercial development in the public sector
David Elverson

Copyright © 2021 David Elverson

Cover Design: Mr Blinc Design

All rights reserved. This book was published by Wild Horses Publishing. No part of this book may be reproduced in any form by any means without the expressed permission of the authors. This includes reprints, excerpts, photocopying, recording or any future means of reproducing text. The only exception is brief quotations in printed reviews.

If you would like to do any of the above please seek permission by contacting the author at www.commercialgov.co.uk

Published in the United Kingdom by Wild Horses Publishing

ISBN 978-0-9932363-5-8

DEDICATION

To the heroes and unsung heroes across the public sector who have worked so hard, tirelessly and selflessly to keep us safe and get this nation back on its feet

CONTENTS

COMMERCIAL GOV

1.

INTRODUCTION

The first edition of this book was written four years ago. That perhaps doesn't seem like a long enough time for things to change dramatically and warrant a second edition. However, the opposite is in fact the truth! Policy changes, high profile failures in the national media, the impact of the pandemic on commercial income and the overall financial position of public sector organisations have all changed the commercial landscape. Perhaps most importantly, four more years of learning across the sector has led to a development of what good commercial practice looks like with new examples of success and best practice. This second edition is designed to reflect that and provide an up to date commentary and guide on how to develop commercially.

Before this pandemic commercial development in the public sector was an increasingly important part of the adaptation and change of public sector organisations to operate effectively in the financial, political and social context in which they exist. Covid-19 has exacerbated the drivers for this change and adaptation with the financial imperative to make and/or save greater than it ever has been, whilst demand and need for services is also increasing. In short, financial self-sufficiency, or as close to it as possible given the nature of the organisation and the services it has a duty to provide, is the goal and commercial development is an increasingly important part of achieving this.

In this second edition we keep much of the content that was in the first edition, but also focus on how the public sector can, and needs to, adapt its commercial approach in the post-covid world we hope to move into soon, or indeed, whether we can wait until then.

Can we wait for post-covid?

History teaches us that the businesses that thrive after tumultuous market conditions are in fact those that adapted best during the crisis. This can be seen in modern history looking back to the great depression of the 1930s, the Second World War and more recently, the banking crisis. Businesses that worked hard, understood the environment they were in, how that impacted on their market and adapted during the crisis were far more successful than those who waited for the crisis to be over before responding to it.

The same will be true in this pandemic. Businesses that adapt and respond during this crisis will be the ones that do best afterwards. By continually adapting, the business is in fact ensuring it is in alignment with market needs, whatever those needs are and however they change. This means as our market needs change again as we move from the pandemic into different phases of recovery, those businesses will already know how the market is responding and will be relevant to emerging needs. Businesses that don't adapt during the pandemic will be playing catch up in a fast-moving recovery environment and run the risk of never regaining their market relevance.

The same is true for public sector commercial activity. If the public sector waits until the pandemic is over before refocusing and adapting their commercial approach they run a high risk of 'missing the market' and being locked into a cycle of trying to catch up – a cycle that drains cashflow rather than generates the income that is so needed.

The challenge is greater for the public sector as their workload has increased enormously during the pandemic as part of the emergency response. However, we see a big divide between organisations – those that are 'parking' commercial development until after the crisis is over and those who see commercial development as even more important now and are doing what they can to re position themselves to be commercially relevant in this season and ready for success in the next.

If waiting until we move into a post-covid world means reduced commercial performance not just now, but for the next three to five years, can the public sector afford to do that?

Stories of Success

Throughout this book I will share stories from organisations like yours: success stories and ones where it hasn't turned out so well! I won't mention the names of the organisations, but if there are examples you would like to learn from in more depth then please do contact me and I can put you in touch with clients of mine.

The aim of this book is to support you on this journey; both for you personally and for your organisations. The book is a mixture of theory and practical examples all of which have been refined over the last twenty years to provide you with a process, tools and areas of development that really do work.

As you get into the book the workbook style will help you to explore areas such as:

- What do we mean by 'commercial' and what language is most helpful

- Commercial objectives and the link to corporate strategy

- Focusing in a way that achieves objectives

- Customers and building around them not around our services

- The competitive environment

- Investment

- Innovation

- Commercial Place shaping

- Understanding the bottom line

- Understanding how to position yourself in a market

- Brand

- Implementation: system, structure and process

- Implementation: people and culture

- Risk

- Corporate parenting – setting it up so you are most likely to derive the benefits you are looking for

It only takes a small number of people with enthusiasm, drive and resilience to create the critical mass needed to drive new thinking and working practices across an organisation. This small group can actual create substantial and lasting change must quicker than you might expect. Great commercial results are possible, it just requires some new ideas, a can do attitude and an organisational savviness to understand who and how to influence others to join this journey.

WHAT DOES 'BEING COMMERCIAL' MEAN?

Words can be very powerful and often convey different meanings to different people; often not the intended meaning. This is definitely the case with the language around commercialisation. The word 'commercial' has many different meanings and leads to confusion whilst other associated words such as 'marketing', 'sales' and 'profit' also have numerous definitions and often create many negative connotations in the minds of staff. Being clear on the language of commercialisation is an important first step.

In my experience the word 'commercial' is largely being used in three different contexts in the public sector:

- Income generation

- Efficiency and effectiveness

- Contract management

It can quite rightly be used in all of these contexts, but using the same word to describe all three leads to confusion and lack of focus.

An important first task is to determine the language of commercialisation that you are going to use and stick with it across your organisation. One of my local authority clients has actually banned the word 'commercial' and instead uses 'income generation' when talking about that, 'efficiency and effectiveness' when that is the focus or 'contract management' when discussing creating 'commercially' minded relationships with partners and suppliers.

Activity: - My definition of 'commercial'.

When using the word 'commercial' I mean.....

We work with the widest possible definition of commercial and have been involved in projects across the public sector where commercial is defined as:

income generation　　*efficiency*

asset utilisation　　*contract management*

innovation　　*place shaping*

market management

THE ESSENCE OF BEING COMMERCIAL

'Being commercial' is to hold two elements in tension. On the one hand we must be innovative, creative and see things differently than we have before. However this must be held in tension with having good, solid, robust processes. Both are needed and when the approach to commercial development veers too far to either end of this spectrum it is very easy to make mistakes that lead to wasted time, effort, reputation, money and perhaps most importantly, the emotional good will of staff.

INNOVATIVE / CREATIVE   ROBUST PROCESS

BEING COMMERCIAL

To slightly over exaggerate, I have seen many car crashes at both ends of this spectrum. When an organisation veers too far to the creative and innovative at the expense of process, activities are undertaken that should never have started. A generalised example would be as follows:

A director somewhere has a bright idea and thinks; "we can make loads of money if we...". The analysis of the idea against customer requirements, the competitive environment and the capability to deliver consistently is never undertaken thoroughly and investment is put into something that fails and probably should never have started.

At the other end of the spectrum I could recount countless examples where process is used at the expense of creativity and innovation. When this happens either the ideas aren't generated in the first place, or if they are, bureaucracy kicks in and creates so many hoops to jump through that nothing ever materialises and certainly not in a timely fashion with the motivation of staff still intact.

I used to be the Commercial Director of a consultancy that had a strategy of recruiting ex-directors and heads of service from public sector organisations. They did this knowing that relationships are very important in winning consultancy assignments and the little black book of contacts these individuals had was of great value. These ex-directors clearly fell into two categories. With the first group you could visibly see the chains fall off as they realised they had the freedom and authority to make decisions without having to write numerous reports and go to several committees to get approval for a minor decision. The second group I called the Shawshank Redemption group. They had strong similarities to Red, Morgan Freeman's character in the film. When Red was released from prison he couldn't cope in the outside world because he was institutionalised. These senior, intelligent and highly professional people fell into this group. They had become so used to thinking a certain way that they weren't able to adapt and think differently. It can be the same for us as we look to work differently. Many of these ex-directors had become so used to certain ways of working and thinking that they couldn't cope with the freedoms that came, and are needed, to operate commercially.

This illustrates a very important aspect of 'being commercial'. Our mind set is probably more important than our skill set. Many of the issues I encounter when supporting organisations in their commercial development are nothing to do with not having 'commercial capability'. They are more to do with the culture of the organisation; a culture that does not encourage individuals to think in ways that foster creativity and innovation.

To lead the change we need to not only buy into it ourselves, but know how to win the hearts and minds of staff. Ultimately it is they who make new commercial initiatives work, often whilst doing the 'day job' at the same time.

Most of the rest of this book focuses on the processes needed to develop commercially, but the process only works if the ideas are there in the first place; that requires innovation.

As you read the rest of this book I encourage you to consciously look beyond the ways things work at the moment, as it is only when we do this that we can identify the, as yet unrealised, potential. The potential then needs to be processed to turn it into the possible.

OPPORTUNITIES

I have worked with many public sector organisations to set up income generation initiatives and have seen and worked with many more that were already in existence. They can be categorised into three main types:

- Asset based initiatives

- Value based initiatives

- Competence based initiatives

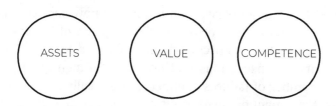

Asset based initiatives are ones where the organisation has a particular asset that it uses to create an income. The most obvious example of this would be a building that is no longer needed due to staff rationalisation and is let to other businesses; generating rental income. Sometimes the asset used is the reserves. The reserves are used to 'buy' an income generating opportunity such as housing, that is sold or rented to create income. In one fairly well known example a local authority bought a hotel with their cash assets as it was seen as a good investment opportunity.

Value based initiatives look at an existing services and identify and exploit value that currently isn't passed on to the customer. An interesting example of this comes from the world of food hygiene. A local authority did a survey of the food outlets in their area and asked them what food hygiene rating they would like. Unsurprisingly the majority came back to them and said they would like five stars. The team then sent all food outlets in their area a letter six months prior to their next inspection. In this letter they offered them an audit with a clear action plan which, if followed, would result in five stars at the re-inspection. Many of the food outlets took them up on this because they recognised the value to their business of this service. It created value in four ways:

1. Income was generated for the local authority by the fee paid for the audit service. Not a huge amount, but income nevertheless.

2. The local authority also found the new service created efficiency gains for them. The majority of the workload is spent on enforcing changes when a food outlet fails and on inspections that are not of a high quality. The number of failures dropped dramatically and in fact the time spent on inspections also decreased as food outlets were more prepared for them and they were of a higher quality.

3. The food businesses of the area were delighted with the service as they found it helped them increase their competitiveness.

4. Value was created for the general public as the standard and safety of food in the area increased.

I have shared this example with many local authorities. Many hear the story and are surprised at how easy it was for this local authority and are motivated to go away and do something similar. Others hear the story and their starting point is to see all of the potential problems: "there's a conflict of interest there, how can you provide an audit service and still be the regulator?" "Sounds great but we don't have the resources to do that".

I'm not saying all local authorities should do this. However the reaction to the story illustrates the mind set challenges I mentioned. To effectively move the commercial development agenda forward we need a mind-set of 'what is possible' rather than one of getting stuck at the first barriers.

Interestingly I have come across another local authority that has run an almost identical service that hasn't worked at all. The main difference is the language used to describe the service. They called it a *'mentoring service'* rather than an audit. This illustrates a problem at the other end of the spectrum – not enough of a robust process. This service made an assumption that client didn't want the 'hard regulatory' side of the council to provide a service but would prefer a soft 'hand-holding' approach. This assumption was never tested and the resulting service failed. In this particular example the value to the customer came from the fact it was the regulator providing the service and that an audit leaves nothing unsaid. They would get a list of everything they needed to do before their next inspection. A robust process to test the assumption and combine it with the good idea would have resulted in a much more successful outcome.

Competence based initiatives are where a particular skill, knowledge, process or combination of these is used to provide a new service for other customers. An example of this would be the payroll service of an organisation offering payroll to small businesses or other public sector bodies.

Competence based initiatives are a common area of income generation in local authorities and often revolve around training and consultancy services. However it is also one of the hardest to make work well and there are potential pitfalls in doing this that we will explore later.

THE MARKETING LENS

There are many different ways of looking at what it means to be commercial. A lens that I find useful for looking at the key components of it is marketing, or more accurately strategic marketing. There are many definitions as to what marketing is. One I particularly like comes from the American Marketing Association:

Marketing is finding out what your customers [stakeholders] want, positioning your product or service to meet that need and communicating your superior customer value.

There are three key parts to this definition:

- Market research

- Product or service development

- Promotional activity

MARKET RESEARCH	PRODUCT DEVELOPMENT	PROMOTION

I've trained over 4000 public sector managers in commercial awareness over the last five of years. I always get them to work in groups to define marketing. All of them include promotional activity in their definitions. About 40% include market research; finding what customers actually want, and about 10% include product or service development in the definitions. However all three aspects are vitally important.

MARKET RESEARCH - WHAT CUSTOMERS REALLY WANT

To be commercially aware means to understand who our customers are, understand what they are after and build our offering around them, not around us. I reckon about 90% of the public sector income generation initiatives I have come across start from the position of; *'here is something we do, lets flog it to make some money'*. Quite possibly they are good at providing whatever the internal service is and possibly there could be a market for it, however the mind-set is wrong. It is focussed on building something you have rather than finding out if there is a need. Another way of looking at it is that this mind set is really saying *'we have a problem, how can we find customer to solve that problem for us'*. This is the wrong way round. We need to understand the problems and needs customers have and align our services to solve their problems. Without flipping this mindset around we won't create the long term sustainable businesses that are needed to meet the aspirations I come across frequently such as 'we want to be self-sufficient and not rely on central government grants'.

When good market analysis is done well it moves beyond looking at what customers say they want. One of Henry Ford's famous quotes was; *'if I gave people what they said they wanted*

I'd have invented faster horses'. People don't always know what is possible. We need to combine an understanding of what they want and their expectations with what we know is possible.

This stage is vitally important. The focus becomes on putting the customer first and centring everything we do around them rather than around us. A rather trite test of this is to look at an organisation's website. Is the menu structure based around their internal departments or what the customer is looking for?

This is a challenge for the private sector just as much as the public. Throughout this book I will use private sector examples as well as ones taken from the public sector. I do this because a sentiment I come across fairly frequently is 'we need to be more like the private sector'. I'm not a big fan of thinking like this because what is the private sector anyway? There is the big and the small, the good and the bad, the ethical and the unethical etc.

A friend of mine runs a digital consultancy business that helps companies focus on their website users. He worked with one of the big insurance companies to focus the web site for one of their main insurance products more on the customer experience and journey. The result was a reduction in the time it took for a customer to buy the insurance by around 40%, increased satisfaction and greater profitability.

The challenge in whatever sector we are in is the same – we need to focus around the customer with them being the expert rather than around us and what we do.

An illustration of this can be found by looking at most local authority planning departments. Pretty much all local authorities who are developing commercially have done something about charging for pre-application advice particularly for major planning developments. However from the customer's perspective they want a one-stop shop. They don't care that planning is a different department from building control, which is different again from environmental health. They don't care that highways is actually controlled by a different council altogether. A pre-application service that focuses on the customer hides any departmental and hopefully organisational boundaries from the customer and provides a seamless holistic service.

PRODUCT OR SERVICE DEVELOPMENT

From the position of understanding what customers need or want we can now tweak, develop or possibly revolutionise what we are doing to make sure our products or services fit that need.

PROMOTIONAL ACTIVITY

Now we understand what customers want and we have developed our offering to take that into account, the promotional activity is about telling a story: we listened to you, we've changed things as a result and here you are, something that meets your needs. This approach fits strongly with the values of the public sector as it is pretty much the same process as developing and delivering a good public service. Because of the synergy with public sector values, this approach helps to get staff on board and is a building block to the creation of a strong brand, something that we will cover later on in this book.

A SHORT HISTORY LESSON

A good way to describe the journey needed to commercialise public sector services is to look at the development of businesses since the industrial revolution. In the early days businesses were product led. They had a product and customers could take it or leave it. Ford is a great example of this – *'you can have it in any colour as long as it's black'*.

Businesses then became sales led. They continued to have the same product but became better at selling those products. They sold harder, they began to understand the emotions involved with purchasing decisions and to use them to their advantage and generally pushed their products hard. There are many businesses who still adopt this approach today.

The most sophisticated businesses are market and customer led. They follow the process outlined earlier: they identify need, alter what they are doing as result of these findings and communicate the value they have created.

PRODUCT LED

SALES LED

MARKET AND CUSTOMER LED

This spectrum of development is the same one public sector organisations are navigating. An example of this can be seen by looking at a client of mine; a school improvement service.

This service has traditionally provided support services to schools such as HR, ICT, payroll and professional development services. In the past schools had to use them which led to a product led mind set in the service: *"this is what we do, take it or leave it, because you can't go anywhere else anyway"*! As a short aside I think it is easy to spot a product led mind-set by looking at the main form of marketing communications. If they use a brochure then I reckon they are product led. *"Here you are. Here is everything we offer you might find something you need in there"*.

The world then changed for this service. Schools were given more autonomy and could go to different providers. New types of schools emerged such as Academies and Free Schools which had even greater levels of autonomy. New providers came into the market place who adopted a market and customer led approach. They worked closely with the Headteachers and other key staff to develop real relationships and flexible models of delivery that were based around the requirements of the schools. The service I was working with was getting blown out of the water – not because they weren't good and their staff weren't professional, in fact they were great, but because their approach, their mind set, wasn't putting the customer first.

To change this required some process change, to develop better relationships and understand customer needs; however the main change was in their mind set. They had to move from a mind-set of *'we are the experts this is what you need'* to a mind-set of *'you are the experts, how can we support you'*.

It is a subtle change, but has an enormous impact.

A SPLIT CULTURE

The challenge for public sector organisations, particularly local authorities, is that two different cultures are now needed in the one organisation. For commercial initiatives to succeed a market and customer led culture is required, whilst for traditional services, particularly regulatory ones with statutory duties, a product led culture is still required. This means for the public sector to deliver everything the new world requires of them they must create an approach that enables both cultures to co-exist. This is a challenge, although not a unique one. Take Apple as an example. In their manufacturing department they create a culture of absolute standardisation with zero tolerance of defects. However in their R&D department they create a culture that encourages risks to be taken and boundaries to be pushed. Both of these cultures co-exist within the same organisation.

The challenge is new for public sector organisations and sits at the heart of what must be accomplished for the new commercial challenges to be met head on whilst maintaining traditional services.

A FRAMEWORK FOR DEVELOPING COMMERCIALLY

The following framework has been implemented in many different public sector organisations to structure and focus the commercial development activities. It includes the main areas that must be thought through before commercial initiatives are launched and also provides an evaluation process for existing initiatives. Later on in the book I will mention how different organisations implement such a structure, but for now we will briefly introduce it before the majority of the rest of the book goes through each stage in more details with exercises for you to complete to make it real and useful for the commercial development of your organisation.

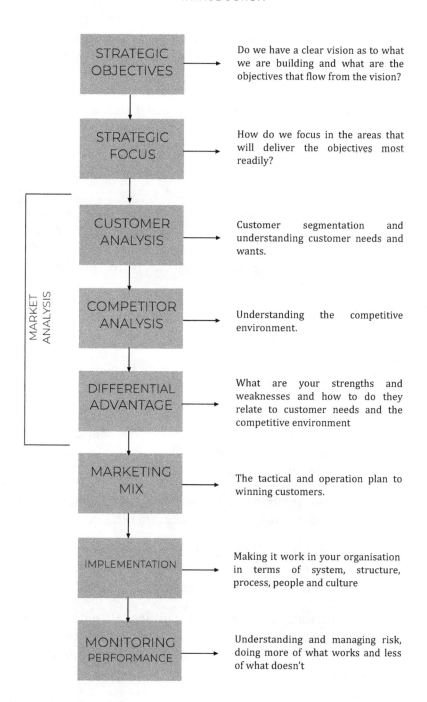

STRATEGIC OBJECTIVES — Do we have a clear vision as to what we are building and what are the objectives that flow from the vision?

STRATEGIC FOCUS — How do we focus in the areas that will deliver the objectives most readily?

CUSTOMER ANALYSIS — Customer segmentation and understanding customer needs and wants.

COMPETITOR ANALYSIS — Understanding the competitive environment.

DIFFERENTIAL ADVANTAGE — What are your strengths and weaknesses and how to do they relate to customer needs and the competitive environment

MARKETING MIX — The tactical and operation plan to winning customers.

IMPLEMENTATION — Making it work in your organisation in terms of system, structure, process, people and culture

MONITORING PERFORMANCE — Understanding and managing risk, doing more of what works and less of what doesn't

MARKET ANALYSIS

1. **Strategic objectives, what are you trying to achieve**. We all know good management practice is to have a vision and clear objectives. In a high proportion of the commercial initiatives I come across these are missing or the objectives are no more than *'being cost neutral'*. To create long term sustainable income generating initiatives we need a vision as to what we are building that is aspirational for staff. We also need clear objectives that flow from this.

2. **Focus**. Having ideas is never the problem. Choosing which ones are most likely to deliver against the objectives and sticking to them is a must greater challenge. To be commercially aware we need to be focused and intentional.

3. **Customers**. We need to understand who our customers are and what they want.

4. **Competitive environment** – we need to understand the nature of the competitive environment we are operating in.

5. **Differential advantage** – we need to understand our strengths and weaknesses and how they relate to what customer want and what competitors are doing.

6. **The marketing mix** – this is where the tactical marketing plans come into play, turning ideas into reality.

7. **Implementation – system, structure and process**. How do we implement our commercial initiatives in a way that maximises the chance for success?

8. **Implementation – people and culture**. How do we win staff's hearts and minds and create an environment where people are motivated and excited by the commercial journey?

The next few chapters take you through the framework, base the exercises on a real commercial opportunities or existing initiatives. It could be one you are already working on, one that is coming up soon or an idea that you have for the future. It is important to turn theory into reality so I encourage you to spend time completing the activities as it will give you the draft outline of a commercial plan and turn reading a good book into a rich learning journey!

2.

STRATEGIC OBJECTIVES

We all know that standard good management practice is to have a vision of where we are heading and from that key objectives will flow. We know this is important because we need to inspire others working on whatever it is we are doing with a vision and we need to manage and monitor our progress towards it through objectives. We all know that and we do that for our general 'business as usual'. However in my experience this is an area that is largely forgotten about or ignored when developing public sector businesses or income generation opportunities.

Nine times out of ten there isn't a vision or if there is it is no more compelling that *'we need to be cost neutral'*! A vision like that isn't going to inspire staff to roll their sleeves up and put extra effort into doing the day job and working hard to make something new work at the same time. This is often the reality; income generation opportunities rely on staff doing them on top of the day job in the early days, so understanding and applying basic motivational principles is an absolute must.

Part of the reason there isn't a vision is because the mind set often doesn't move beyond the short term. There is an immediate budgetary pressure so the focus of income generation just looks at the short term. This, whilst being understandable, is not the sort of approach that will help the public sector develop long term sustainable income streams that help them to invest back into front line services.

Without medium to long term strategic objectives and a vision to point them in the right direction, all that will happen is the commercial development approach will move from one short term opportunity to the next, staff will join in half-heartedly and nothing major will be achieved. The need for a vision is paramount.

Activity

Imagine you are a journalist five years in the future writing an article about what has been achieved over the last five years by the income generation opportunity / business you are focusing on. Include the 'good' that has been achieved, but also include business information such as; how much turnover, how much profit, where is it operating geographically etc.

This activity helps you to think about the future and focus on what you want to build. What will it look like, who will be working in it, how many people, what services will you be providing and for whom? How much will you be turning over and how much profit will you be bringing back to the parent organisation?

We need to think about these things so we know what we are aiming for and building. We need to have a compelling story to inspire our staff with that is more than the fear tactics I come across so often which are along the lines of *we need to be cost neutral to save our jobs*. Whilst this might be the reality of the situation it is such a limiting vision. It does not inspire staff with what might be possible and therefore doesn't result in emotional engagement with the idea to build something sustainable. Instead it reiterates the short term nature of the mind-set and reduces the impact.

This approach, which is so prevalent, in fact could be much more detrimental. I read some research a few years ago that looked at people's productivity in the workplace. It found that during a typical eight hour working day an average employee is productive for five and a half of the eight hours. During times of high stress that time of being productive dropped to less than one hour. Working on something new and doing new things, such as selling, in order to save your job certainly creates a high stress situation. I've seen first morale and then productivity drop in such environments on so many occasions. Of course the reality is that without success jobs are at risk, but this is no different to any business. We need visions that focus on the medium to long term and what we are building. This then inspires staff and gives them a reason to put the effort in, whatever the context and the circumstances.

To be commercially aware is to understand how to win the hearts and minds of staff and take them on the journey. They are the ones who will make our commercial initiatives succeed. Vision is central to this because vision gives people purpose. Deriving a sense of purpose in what we do and why we do it is so important. Finding meaning and having a vision that we are working towards motivates us and often gives us the strength to keep on going, even if things seem tough.

THE REASON FOR A VISION

I've recently been involved in the merger of three large social care organisations. They are all well-known brands and were merged to form a market leader in the UK. My specific involvement was in the post-merger culture change work to try and forge a single organisation in the place of three different ones operating under the same brand.

The new company had a markedly different purpose than two of the original companies. This had a very obvious effect on the staff, both for good and bad. On the positive side, the lead company in the merger, and the one under whose brand name the new organisation traded, was a well-respected brand that stands for quality. This company expects a quality service and this is underpinned through a comprehensive set of values that articulates expectations for each job role in the organisation. The purpose of providing a high end, quality and respected service had an effect on the staff from the other two companies. They were influenced positively by being associated with the purpose of this brand.

The merger also had a more negative impact. The focus of the leading brand was to work with a wealthy set of clients in order to create greater shareholder value. This was very different to the historic client group of the other two companies. Traditionally they had worked with clients who received state help to pay for their care needs. There was an interesting and marked difficulty for the staff from the other two companies to buy into the vision of the leading brand. The meaning many staff had found; in providing important services to those who couldn't afford them any other way, was being challenged. Their meaning was no longer in alignment with the purpose of the new organisation.

This alignment, or lack of alignment, is important to think about before considering what vision is, because our visions can either bring people to life or have the opposite effect. This is often the case when the public sector develops commercially as there is a perception that the very nature of the organisation is changing and moving away from a public service ethos.

Have you ever been in a situation where what you were hearing and seeing was so different to your experiences that it actually made you feel stressed? A slightly harder question to answer, because it happens more subtly is; have you ever noticed yourself creating justifications to explain things that are at odds with what you are seeing and experiencing? And on reflection, noticed that the justifications are more unbelievable than the original event you are trying to justify?

The banking crisis badly affected many of the clients of the consultancy I was working for at the time. We were a small, but highly respected boutique consultancy that specialised in small to medium sized change projects with public sector organisations. Over a period of about three months these jobs seemed to dry up. Clients weren't looking for small consultancy projects; they were now looking for whole organisational change programmes and wanted the trusted name of one of the big five to deliver the work for them.

The change happened so quickly that it was at complete odds with our experience. Up until that point business had been good and growing rapidly. Over the course of a few months that had changed considerably. These events were in such a contrast to our experiences of the previous three years that some of our justifications and predictions for what the market would do were actually far more unbelievable than the truth; the market had significantly changed and we had to survive.

A really interesting piece of work was undertaken by Leon Festinger in the 1950s that explains these natural human reactions. His work, the theory of cognitive dissonance, showed that humans strive for internal consistency. When inconsistency (dissonance) is experienced, individuals can become psychologically distressed, or stressed as we would call it. His work led him to two key hypotheses:

- "The existence of dissonance (inconsistency with experiences and world view), being psychologically uncomfortable, will motivate the person to try to reduce the dissonance and achieve consonance"

- "When dissonance is present, in addition to trying to reduce it, the person will actively avoid situations and information which would likely increase the dissonance"

This means we find experiences that are at odds with our previous experiences and expectations stressful and try to avoid them.

He also found that the amount of dissonance, or inconsistency, and the subsequent stress is dependent on an interesting variable:

- *The importance*: The more the experience is valued, the greater the dissonance and stress.

This means that 'dissonance' or stress is particularly prevalent when the event we are experiencing is at odds with something that we value. An example of this would be someone who had very strong environmental values working at an unethical mining company whose inherent values were to exploit the environment. The values of the individual would be very different to the formal and particularly informal values of the mining company, thus creating inconsistency and leading to high levels of stress.

The work my firm and others have done in the field of engagement has demonstrated the impact of alignment of values. The meaning and purpose a person has, and in particular its alignment to the formal and informal values, purpose and vision of the organisation the person is a part of, has a large impact on how engaged someone is. Dan Pink, in his excellent book Drive, came to the same conclusion. He identified three factors that influence our intrinsic motivation; autonomy, mastery and purpose. His definition of purpose is very similar to this. He found that we need to have a purpose and we need to see an alignment between that purpose and what we are actually doing at work in order to be motivated.

This is why vision is so important: for people to have a vision and purpose is motivational and brings them alive. We need a vision and we need to lead others in a way so they develop their own vision. When we are leading people we need to realise the impact our vision and underlying values have on those around us. If they are different from their experiences, expectations and values it actually creates dissonance for them, or as we would commonly experience it; stress.

Festinger's theory is also based on an assumption that people seek consistency between their expectations and reality. Because of this, people engage in a process called dissonance reduction to bring their thoughts, expectations and actions in line with one another. This creation of uniformity allows for less stress.

This reduction can happen in four different ways. Let's have a look at how this plays out in an everyday situation:

Imagine you decided to go on a diet and you are going to avoid high fat foods; however you are in a supermarket and you smell some freshly cooked doughnuts. You buy a doughnut and eat it. Here there is an immediate dissonance; you plan to avoid fatty foods but you find yourself eating a doughnut. The four ways we can reduce this dissonance are as follows:

1. Change our behaviour - we stop eating the doughnut remembering how important it is that we avoid fatty foods.

2. Justify behaviour by changing the conditions - "I'm allowed to eat a doughnut once in a while."

3. Justify behaviour by adding new conditions - "I'll spend 30 extra minutes at the gym to work it off."

4. Ignore/deny any information that conflicts with existing beliefs -"I did not eat that doughnut. I always eat healthily."

Which one of these four reactions do you find yourself falling into? Knowing the way our minds work is important so that we can purposefully operate, think and act in the way we want to, not the way we end up doing. I think most of us have tendencies to one or more of these reactions and our tendency is often a learnt behaviour from our childhood.

The reason I'm writing about cognitive dissonance is because it is so important to understand the impact our vision and values have on those we lead. It is also useful to understand why we react to situations in the way that we do.

Understanding this powerful effect of the human mind allows us to lead in a way that builds a united team, empowers others and ultimately creates motivated people who are happy in work and performing better.

If our vision and values are at odds with the personal vision and values of those we lead it will create a dissonance in them that they will react to in different ways.

The move to more commercial ways of working can create a dissonance for staff. They can perceive the values of the organisation changing and that their purpose, of providing a good public service, is no longer the priority. We need to engage staff in the vision to see that the values haven't changed, it is just a different business model for delivering a public service. In fact I believe it is important to strengthen the public sector values as these are also the area of potential competitive advantage. We will cover this more on the chapter on branding later on in the book.

WHAT COMMERCIAL MEANS TO US

As has already been mentioned in the previous chapter, 'commercial' can mean many different things and there are many different 'commercial' projects that deliver different outcomes. The common thread between all commercial initiatives is they are centred around customers and their needs rather than our services. In this section I expand on some of the types of commercial initiatives with examples from across the public sector to help provide both a definition and hopefully inspiration from good practice across the country.

income generation - the most common form of commercial initiative across the public sector. They centre around using assets (including access to preferential borrowing), competence or value to generate revenue. In a recent series of training workshops I've undertaken for the LGA, around 80% of the 200 delegates said this was the focus of their commercial development.

efficiency - the text book definition of efficiency is our ability to turn inputs into outputs with the least resources and in the quickest manner. There has been a big drive for this in the public sector since the 2008 banking crisis. However, this narrow definition of efficiency has led to salami slicing services to the extent where there isn't the resource available to now grow. In fact a short term approach to savings has hindered the organisations long term ability to operate effectively.

Perhaps what is needed is a focus on cost effectiveness rather than efficiency. Cost effectiveness measures how effectively we turn inputs into impact as described in the diagram below:

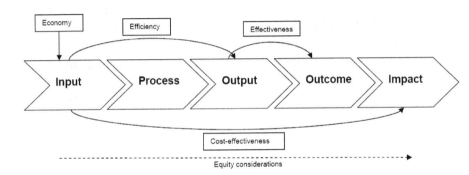

Ultimately it is by delivering better outcomes and impact that we will reduce the cost of the the most expensive public sector services and, in so doing, we will also see greatest improvements for communities across the country.

For example a local authority could make a few hundred thousand through an income generation initiative, but if three new looked after children enter the social care system the income generated will completely disappeared straight away. To be commercial in this area means looking at demand management - how do we manage the demand coming into our expensive systems? Can we reduce demand by working more closely and funding community led organisations? How can we prevent expensive 'events' such as fires happening by front loading the system?

asset utilisation - as the phrase suggests this is about making sure assets are being used to the best possible advantage. This could be land assets or building assets. There are many examples of public sector organisations re purposing their office space to provide the best flexible accommodation for their staff whilst also creating space for rental or conversion to housing.

The timing of the asset utilisation is also important. We are currently working with a local authority that has identified 32 land assets that aren't being utilised. A process was under way to work through them, one at a time, and develop a plan for the land whether it is sale, development or something else. We undertook a cost benefit analysis to show that adding resource to the team and accelerating the work will have a major financial benefit. That benefit will be added to further through the creation of a development business through which the council will keep the majority of the potential the assets have.

contract management - there are major commercial benefits to be had by reducing third party spend and ensuring contracts work in the favour of the public sector purchaser rather than the supplier. This is a large subject area in its own right. There are great examples of public sector organisations doing the following to create major financial and quality benefits:

- creating a category management approach

- shared procurement across the public sector to create economies of scale

- creating a cohort of highly trained negotiators to negotiate major contracts across all service areas

- upskilling contract managers to create 'intelligent client' functions within the organisation that manage contract more effectively

innovation - we all know the need for new innovative approaches that embrace digital and technological advances and create a step changes in the way services are delivered. However, innovation rarely happens by accident and the most innovative companies are very intentional about driving innovation. For more information on this read the chapter on innovation later in the book.

place shaping - regeneration and the development of local areas is sometimes a very commercial activity beyond the role of improving communities. It can lead to increased business rates, but also long term yield for local authorities. There are some great examples where local authority infrastructure such as broadband, is being built into regeneration initiatives, providing a great service for future businesses and residents, but also guaranteeing future income. Recent government changes to Public Works Loan Board (PWLB) borrowing will also make regeneration the focus of borrowing as borrowing for yield won't be allowed. However borrowing for regeneration that then creates yield will be! More information on this can be found in the chapter on investment.

market management - public sector bodies are often large and their purchasing power enables them to influence the market for the good of the communities they serve. We have been involved in a number of projects where this approach creates large savings as well as ensuring a better service is provided in the local area. The mechanism is often a wholly owned limited company. This gives the organisation the chance to drive up quality and drive down price by operating in particular markets. Two examples of this in action from projects I've been involved in:

The creation of a 'flying squad' approach in social care where a small peripatetic multi-skilled team can be set up to operate where commissioners have 'the greatest pain'. That is areas where either the quality of supply is bad or where there is a monopoly that has driven price up. The mere presence of a local authority owned business in the market either drives quality up and price down or the work is given to the flying squad to deliver. This can save millions of pounds when scaled up over a large social care department.

There was a single taxi firm in a market town which led to very high prices for school taxis. The local authority set up its own taxi firm, just to work in a very limited geography and to focus on public sector contracts. This reduced cost dramatically by bringing choice into the market.

BEING FUTURE FOCUSED

Some businesses are very successful at spotting an opportunity, quickly making the most of it and then moving onto the next opportunity. I'd argue that this isn't typically in the DNA of public sector organisations and therefore isn't the approach they should adopt to developing commercially. The public sector is geared up for the medium to long term so this should also be the approach to developing commercially.

In order to do that there has to be a focus on the future operating environment for the business. There is no point creating something for today when everything is going to change tomorrow and we won't be ready for the market until the day after tomorrow!

A great model to help us think about the future operating environment is PESTLE analysis. This is probably something you are familiar with and helps to make the point that commercial development isn't that new or difficult. PESTLE is an acronym of the key areas of change. By looking at what might change in the future it helps us to make decisions now to prepare for challenges and exploit opportunities.

When completing a PESTLE analysis think beyond election cycles. It is very easy for our thinking to get stuck in these cycles and whilst they are important and they do have a big impact on public sector organisations, the world carries on after them and we need to be prepared for that in advance, whichever colour gets into power locally and nationally.

Activity

Complete a PESTLE analysis for your commercial opportunity

Political
Economic
Socio-cultural
Technological
Legal
Environmental

When we think about the future it is important not to just presume it will follow the same path that we are going along at the moment. This is a problem with a lot of the strategic planning that we undertake. We do great analysis to identify the trends of the past that have led us to the present day and then project those same trends into the future and plan for a future based on the trends of the past.

Statistically the chances of that future occurring are tiny. In fact only a slight deviation in the trend will lead to a different future that we haven't planned for. By definition we then become reactive organisations reacting to a future we haven't planned for.

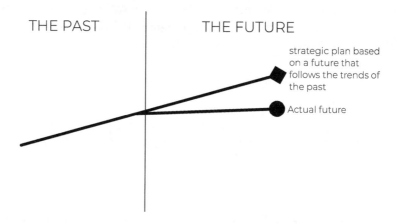

THE PAST   THE FUTURE

strategic plan based on a future that follows the trends of the past

Actual future

This can be illustrated really well by looking at public sector spending. In 2007/8 public sector spending was increasing. Everyone was basing their future plans on that increasing trend of spend carrying on into the future. The banking crisis hit, we entered a period of austerity and suddenly the reality of the future was very different to what had been planned for. Now public sector spending is decreasing rapidly, all plans are based on this decrease continuing and it certainly will for a few years. However how long will that continue and are we ready for when it changes or will we just react when it does?

This is quite an extreme example. The reality is the change in the future can be very small and it still results in a different future to the one we have planned for. We need to move beyond assuming the future will develop in a linear fashion based on the trends of the past. We need to look at what will be driving the future to give us clues as to what the future operating environment might be for the commercial opportunities that we have.

STRATEGIC POSITIONING

An effective commercial outlook is to base what we do around the customer rather than persuade the customer to like what we do. This applies as we develop our strategic objectives. A model that I find very useful for this is the resource and competency matrix from Johnson and Scholes.

	THRESHOLD	UNIQUE
RESOURCES		
COMPETENCIES		

This model says there are certain threshold resources and competencies that we have to have to meet the threshold expectations of the markets we operate in. Threshold expectations are what the customers expect and what the competition will certainly provide. Resources are our assets; buildings, equipment, vehicles and volume of staff. Competencies are our knowledge, skills and processes or ways of working.

Over and above the threshold expectations of the market we might have resources or competencies that are unique; beyond the expectations of customers and exceeding the services or features that competitors are able to provide.

The starting point for using this model is to put yourself in the shoes of your customers. From their perspective not your, what do they expect in terms of resources and competencies?

Activity

Write down the threshold resource and competency expectations of the customers and potential customers of your opportunity

---

In coming up with this list you probably found yourself making many assumptions. Realising when we are making assumptions is an important part of being commercially aware. When we make an assumption we need to check and challenge them to make sure they are right. This needs to be done proportionately to what the consequences would be if the assumption is wrong! If the consequences are small then challenging your assumptions within a team and with a few customers might well be enough. If millions from reserves are being spent then assumptions should be challenged through a formal feasibility study.

Once you have your list of threshold expectations you need to audit yourself against this list, from the customers perspective not yours. Would they say you consistently deliver against those expectations? If not, then doing something about the areas you don't or can't meet expectations is the starting point for a commercial strategy. Not being able to 'tick' one of the expectations is saying that you are not meeting the threshold expectations of the market.

If the opportunity you are using for the activities is just an idea at the moment then the question you need to ask is slightly different: what would we need in place to consistently deliver against the threshold expectations?

Activity

Write down any areas that you struggle to meet threshold expectations consistently

---

I did this exercise with the School Improvement Service I mentioned earlier. They identified the threshold resource and competency requirements of the market and realised they had some gaps; some areas that couldn't consistently meet the threshold expectations. They had a choice at this point: they could decide not to go forward on the commercial development journey, they could look to fill the gaps by developing the resources and competencies needed or they could look to develop a strategic partnership with an organisation that had strengths in the areas that were missing.

They decided to take the last option. The work undertaken became the basis for a specification that went out to the market to identify a strategic partner. One was eventually found and a joint venture was created that has since been very successful.

The same choice is the one that must be made by any organisation that doesn't meet all of the threshold expectations of the market. Doing something about these areas must be the starting point of any commercial strategy as without meeting these expectations success in the market is likely to be limited.

UNIQUE

Over and above the threshold you might have some unique resources or competencies. These are things that are beyond the expectations of customers and that the competition doesn't do. Sometimes these might be linked to the type of organisation you are. For example a local authority offering a food hygiene audit service has a unique competence which is the fact they are also the regulator of the service.

Many unique resources and competencies cost money. There is then an equation that has to be balanced. Does the added value outweigh the cost? If it doesn't the unique feature is not commercially viable and should be stopped.

I was working with a Housing Association that had a feature they considered to be unique and valuable. It was a 24/7 call centre. By all accounts it was unique in the local market, but it cost a lot to run it. It was certainly debatable whether the value created outweighed the cost.

If you have resources and competencies that are unique and give you a competitive advantage then part of your commercial strategy should be looking at ways to protect and maintain the unique features. In the large private sector businesses this is the role of the R&D departments. This can be a challenge as what is unique today becomes threshold tomorrow as customers grow to expect it and the competition finds ways to imitate it.

Over the summer the air conditioning in my wife's car broke. It was a tragedy! We had to fix it because *"how could we cope without air conditioning"*! However when I was a teenager I remember long summer holiday trips to Cornwall and back and air conditioning didn't even exist. When it first began to be introduced to family cars it was a unique feature, a luxury. However as we grew to expect it, it lost its uniqueness and became threshold. Now you wouldn't buy a car without air conditioning.

When we have unique resources and competencies and we decide to position our product or service around this uniqueness then we have to have a strategy for protecting and maintaining that uniqueness, otherwise our competitive advantage will be short lived.

Many very successful businesses don't have any unique resources or competencies, they focus on doing the threshold well. Being unique is not a prerequisite of commercial success, doing the threshold well is. It is a question of positioning, how are you going to position your opportunity? Around certain unique features or by focusing on delivering the threshold consistently?

Activity

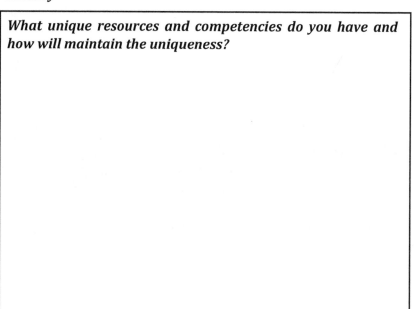

What unique resources and competencies do you have and how will maintain the uniqueness?

It is important to challenge yourself over anything you've listed as unique. In workshops I've had people put things like '*we are responsive and flexible*' as unique. This is absolutely part of threshold and something every customer will expect. How unique are your unique features? Remember that a growing area of competition comes from other public sector organisations. If neighbouring public sector organisations start offering services on your patch then are your services still unique?

It is much better to position yourself to do the threshold well than around unique features if the unique features don't matter that much to the customer. Having a USP is not essential, meeting customer expectations is.

3.

FOCUS

Having ideas and identifying opportunities will not be a problem for you. A far greater challenge is to be focused and intentional in the way you choose which opportunities to pursue and how to follow them through. Some of the opportunities are far more likely to help you achieve your objectives than others and focusing on these is crucial.

A common scenario for many public sector organisations, and therefore managers within these organisations, as they commercialise is the requirement to do their day job at the same time as the new commercial initiatives. This means focusing on the few things that lead to success is even more important.

There are a couple of models that I find useful for focusing on the most important areas. The first of these is Ansoff Matrix:

MARKETS

	EXISTING	NEW
	MARKET PENETRATION	MARKET EXTENSION
	PRODUCT DEVELOPMENT	DIVERSIFICATION

PRODUCTS / SERVICES — EXISTING / NEW

This model shows that we have existing products or services and we have the potential to develop new ones. We also operate in certain markets, but we have the option of expanding into new markets.

If we focus on existing products or services in existing markets this would be a strategy of **market penetration.** An example of this would be a local authority selling payroll services to other local authorities in the local area. This could be the right strategy.

If we decide that our products or services have been so successful that we want to extend them into new markets this would be a strategy of **market extension.** The local authority offering their payroll service in other parts of the country or indeed to a different sector, such as the NHS, would both be examples of this. Both of these could be the right strategy and in fact at the same time as market penetration, however to do either well requires a different focus.

If the local authority decided its core customers wanted a new product or service and developed an associated HR service to go along with the payroll service this would be an example of **product development.** This again might be right and could be run in conjunction with the other two strategies, but again a clearly differentiated approach is needed for this to be successful.

Diversification is where a new product is taken to a new market. This is the highest risk as it is doing something that we haven't done before with people we haven't worked with before. There are some examples of this happening in the public sector that have become quite famous such as the English local authorities that have bought hotels in Scotland.

This model is useful from two perspectives: firstly for the commercial idea itself and secondly as a portfolio management tool to look at all of the commercial opportunities within an organisation.

Within the opportunity there are two important questions: are there clearly differentiated strategies for each of the four areas and what is the right mix for the given time?

Many if not most of the public sector managers I work with identify many opportunities. What often happens is they do a bit of this and a bit of that and a bit of something else and before long they are spread very thin and just end up doing 'stuff'. To be commercially aware is to be focused and intentional. If market extension is right, is it right now? How are we going to go about it? How does our strategy need to differ from market penetration? This focused approach to determining which opportunities to pursue is so important when resources are stretched and the day job needs doing at the same time.

Activity

What percentage of your effort should be in each quadrant now? Is that the case and do you have a clearly differentiated strategy for each activity in each quadrant?

An example of this in action comes from a project I worked on with a local authority a number of years ago. As part of a wider piece of work to develop a commercial approach across the authority, I worked with their Pest Control unit, using them as a pilot project for the rest of authority. This was a small unit with three staff plus the management structure above them. They had a couple of years in which to turn the service around to become cost neutral as it is a non-statutory service which means the council couldn't afford to keep it running at a loss.

The operatives were great at pest control, but didn't know where to start when it came to marketing and growing the business. In the absence of a clear strategy they actually followed the product development route, although they didn't know this is what they were doing! They were struggling to win the commercial pest control contracts they wanted and therefore had spare capacity. To fill that capacity they found a gap in the house clearance market. This earned them some short term income, but also took up any spare capacity thereby reducing their ability to develop their core business of pest control.

The strategy we developed focused on their core business as it was the commercial pest control contracts that had the potential to generate more significant income streams. To begin with the strategy was to focus on market penetration. That is to focus on the commercial contracts in the local area. The commercial contracts are more lucrative and are largely planned preventative work which made resourcing and staffing them easier.

After a period of success in this area they then moved on to look at market extension whilst maintaining a focus on increasing market share in their existing patch. Quite a few of the neighbouring authorities had disbanded their pest control service which created an opportunity. Focusing initially on geographical areas close to the district and again on commercial contracts they expanded into new geographical areas, eventually developing some new hubs outside their own district which further aided the continued geographical expansion.

Once they were established and developed in their core business they then started to look at product development. They identified a gap in the market for pigeon proofing buildings and successfully expanded into this market as well.

So they did go down a route of product development but at the right time and in the right way from a position of strength and with a clear strategy for doing so. When they started with a strategy of product development, it took their attention away from where success would come from. Later on, from a position of strength it then became right. Timing and focus is everything.

This matrix is also useful as a portfolio management tool. Is there the right mix of commercial opportunities across the organisation? If the majority of opportunities are in the top half of the matrix then there is probably short term income being generated but how long will it last? Are there product recycling strategies in place to ensure you are always meeting customer expectations? If the matrix is bottom heavy then it is probably costing money at the moment and there is a risk that it won't generate the expected returns.

The second model I use in this area is to look at the critical success factors and use these to determine where the focus and attention needs to be placed.

Critical Success Factors (CSF) are the small number of things that are most critical to success. It is easy to come up with a list of things that are important; the challenge is to narrow that down to the few that really are critical.

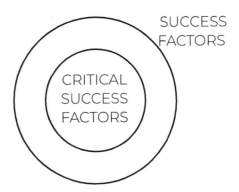

A large charity I was working with on this exercise came up with a list of important factors: saving money, new innovative methods of service delivery to keep up with the competition, reducing cost out of the service to become more competitive and a few others. For them the real CSF however, is the ability to do more with less.

Once you know your CSFs it is time to identify your core competencies. These are the knowledge, skills and processes needed to succeed in a consistent basis on delivering the CSFs. For the charity I mentioned a core competency identified is therefore one of encouraging and driving through innovation.

Focusing on delivering the core competencies well and with consistency will lead to a focused approach with effort put into the most important areas.

Activity

What are your Critical Success Factors and what knowledge, skills and processes are needed to consistently deliver against them?

COMMERCIAL GOV

4.

INNOVATION

Every public sector organisation I've worked with desires innovation. There is a clear understanding that there needs to be new ways of delivering services, new approaches, new process and new technology. The desire is there, yet the level of innovation in the sector doesn't match the desire. There are great examples of innovation, but the systematic delivery of new innovative solutions doesn't meet the aspiration or the demand. That is because innovation rarely happens by accident! In his excellent book 'Be Less Zombie' Elvin Turner describes it as a battle – *'Innovation is an argument inside most companies – frail new ideas versus the overwhelming power of the status quo'*. The status quo in most public sector organisations is very strong, stronger than in many, if not most, other sectors. Therefore the innovative idea, by itself, stands little chance to be accepted as an idea, developed into a business case, piloted, scaled up and implemented as business as usual.

Innovation rarely happens by accident. As Turner says: *'An innovation strategy helps create an environment where new ideas can emerge and thrive. It is the single most important way to build and sustain innovative performance. And it doesn't have to be difficult.'*

It might not have to be difficult, but very few public sector organisations have an innovation strategy. To continue using an analogy Turner uses in his excellent book, the approach to innovation is similar to 'casual dating'. Organisations aren't deliberate about innovation which means efforts evaporate quickly, business as usual is too-busy and too powerful to make room for upstart, inconvenient, unproven and resource-hungry ideas.

The transition from a casual dating mentality to a strategic always on commitment is what sets apart the innovation powerhouses we read about: Amazon, Google, Netflix, Apple, Tesla and the like.

The challenges facing the public sector are great and not going to get any easier in the coming years. We need innovation to help us face these challenges and the only way for that to happen is for each public sector organisation to take innovation seriously with a strategic always-on commitment.

This chapter will only scratch the surface of developing an innovation strategy that delivers results in the public sector. I thoroughly recommend getting a copy of Be Less Zombie for far more information and details about how to make it work and stick, whatever type of organisation yours is and whatever the current culture and approach to innovation. In line with the ethos of this book I'm going to draw out a few of the elements of developing an intentional approach to innovation that I've found to have the largest and quickest impact in the public sector.

An approach to innovation doesn't have to be complex, but it does have to be clear, Incremental ideas for innovation tend to need less process because they typically form part of business-as-usual and can be delivered with existing teams and resources. The more disruptive an idea, the greater the chance resources being wasted, time spent not making decisions and inertia. However, across the public sector leaders tell me it is disruptive innovation that is needed. Through his extensive work across some of the world's most innovative companies, Turner says you will find a very similar, lightweight process in place that follows three essential steps:

Step 1: Finding Opportunities (Customer / Opportunity Fit)

- Identifying the right problems and opportunities

- Designing innovative questions

Step 2: Finding Solutions (Opportunity / Solution Fit)

- Generating ideas

- Assessing and selecting ideas

- Testing assumptions with experiments

- Scaling and integrating experiments

Step 3: Finding Business Models (Solution / Market Fit)

- Identifying viable business models

Turner expands on each stage and the diagram at the end of the chapter demonstrates the way the stages flow together. I'm going to concentrate on just a few of these stages to show how they link to a very common situation we find in public sector organisations and therefore how they can be used to improve the quality of innovative ideas and staff engagement in the process. The following scenario, taken from a recent local authority we've been working, with introduces the problem:

We recently undertook a commercial review of a local authority. They had compiled a list of 97 possible commercial ideas and most of these had been generated through a staff suggestion box – or a virtual equivalent of one. Staff had been asked to come up with their best commercial ideas and submit them. Staff had engaged in this process to begin with and submitted ideas. However, there was disappointment from the commercial team and senior managers about the quality of the ideas. Most of the ideas were about small scale service improvement, a large proportion of them would have probably cost more money than they made and quite a few were definitely not the sort of thing the local authority wanted to get involved with.

Nothing happened with the ideas, the staff who submitted them weren't communicated with, no new commercial initiatives came from the ideas and gradually staff not only disengaged with coming up with new ideas, but with the whole commercial development agenda.

Whilst this was a relatively extreme example, the principles demonstrated in this small scenario are common to so many innovation approaches in the public sector.

The great news is we can make large strides forwards by simply building in some of the stages outlined above:

Identifying the right problems and opportunities

There needs to be guidance parameters put in place before asking staff for their ideas. A good commercial strategy and vision can help with this so there is a common understanding of 'what commercial means to us' across the organisation. This can then guide the thinking of staff so the ideas they generate, even the most disruptive ones, are still within the value base and vision of the organisation.

Designing Innovative Questions

I think this is one of the most commonly missed stages. The questions asked of staff are too wide and generic which means it should be no surprise when the ideas that come back are also wide and generic. Innovation works best when great innovative questions target peoples thinking to specific challenges that need new solutions. As Turner says:

Most brainstorms leave participants underwhelmed and frustrated. Bold ideas are shut down. Small ideas aren't edgy enough. Variations on old ideas come out yet again. And the 'cool' ideas don't actually solve the problem. One of the main causes of a low-voltage brainstorm is a dimly lit starting point.

When catalytic questions emerge a sequence of five important innovation outcomes are activated:

Increased strategic alignment – we provoke ideas whose intended outcomes clearly link back to strategy

More effective outcomes for managers – we calibrate idea generation to deliver the most appropriate kind of ideas

Less frustrating problem solving for staff – everyone is clear on the kind of ideas that we are pitching for, yet we have creative freedom to imagine wide-ranging solutions

More creative ideas – we break the stupefying power of the status quo over our imaginations

Short-term and long-term alignment – we can define some commercial parameters of innovation both now and in the future

The questions we pose set targets and expectations and indicate to staff the level of risk and disruption we might be looking for. For example catalytic questions for incremental innovation might be:

How can we reduce spend by 10% whilst improving the quality of service we are offering?

How can we increase income by £2 million through our operational services?

If we are looking for more disruptive ideas then the catalytic questions also need to communicate that:

How can we stop older people needing social care?

How can we generate enough additional income to completely pay for the schools budget?

These questions may set an impossible task, but they will create the environment for disruptive innovation where the ideas that come forward have the potential to create step changes rather than incremental advances.

Testing assumptions with experiments

Whenever anything new is tried there is no certainty it will succeed due to the many variables at play. This is one of the main reasons the status quo in the public sector is so strong. We are stewarding public money so 'failing' isn't an option and 'speculating' on new innovations is often not viewed as good stewardship. This is true, stewarding public money wisely is very important, but the risk of not trying something new is increasingly becoming as big a risk, if not bigger, than the risk of trying something.

The solution to this is to not to put all of our eggs into one basket, accept there will be failures, but set up new initiatives as experiments with the lowest level of cost and resource possible to test the validity of the new idea. This is called creating a Minimum Viable Product (MVP). This way we are able to develop evidence, intelligence and understanding about likely future success before any scaling occurs.

Innovation is vital to meet the challenges facing the public sector. Our approach to commercial development must embrace innovation as it is only by coming up with new ways of growing commercially that we will achieve the financial rebalancing public sector budget need. Staff in the public sector are just as innovative as staff anywhere else. To harness this we need to be intentional about innovation, develop innovation strategies and have a clear process of innovation so we move from casually dating innovation to a strategic always-on commitment.

Elvin Turner has made many excellent innovation tools available for free at the following website: - https://www.belesszombie.com/resources

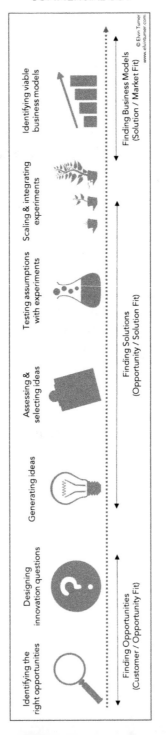

Identifying the right opportunities

Designing innovation questions

Generating ideas

Assessing & selecting ideas

Testing assumptions with experiments

Scaling & integrating experiments

Identifying viable business models

Finding Opportunities (Customer / Opportunity Fit)

Finding Solutions (Opportunity / Solution Fit)

Finding Business Models (Solution / Market Fit)

© Elvin Turner
www.elvinturner.com

5.

CUSTOMERS

Given the definition of marketing I used earlier and the emphasis I've given on building around customers not what you do, it is probably important to spend more time looking at our customers. In order to build around them we need to really understand them!

The starting point for understanding our customers is firstly to recognise they aren't all the same. Customer segmentation is a method that has been around for a long time that helps us to understand the differences our customers have. Some of our language comes from it. Yuppie stands for Young Urban Professional. This tells the marketeers something about their likely disposable income, the amount of free time and their likely interests. This then impacts on the direct mail sent to people in that segment. DINKY is another such segment identified at a national level. This stands for double income no kids. Again this says something about income, time and interests and can therefore direct marketing effort.

Pretty much every successful company will segment its market in some way, shape or form. One company that is very good at it and does it in a very obvious fashion is McDonalds. They know that one of their segments is kids. They have a product especially for them, the Happy Meal and they market it in a specific way linking it to the latest blockbuster kid's films. They know another segment is people grabbing breakfast on the way to work. They have a product especially for them, the bacon and egg McMuffin and they advertise it by focusing on the breakfasts they provide. They know another segment they have; people pretending they are being healthy! They have salads for this segment and they market it with crisp green looking lettuce!

There are very few generic 'we're McDonalds' adverts. Nearly all of them are focused on particular segments. Why? Because by doing that each customer knows there is something for them that meets their needs and that McDonalds understands that need and can satisfy it.

The same approach is needed in our markets as our customers aren't all the same either and have many different needs. If we can group them into distinct groups with similar characteristics then we can create more dynamic and potent relationships with them because we are demonstrating that we understand them and are focusing on them.

The challenge is how to segment the market as there is no one way of doing it. You could segment based on size, geography, socio-demographic characteristics, need or many other characteristics. A friend of mine runs a small charity that houses ex-offenders. He was looking for private landlords to put their property into his scheme. I was helping him out and one of the segments he identified was landlords with a social conscience (apparently they exist!). This is a values based way of segmenting the market.

We work a lot with local authorities. One of the ways we segment the market is on whether or not they are early adopters. By that I mean some local authorities want to be the trail blazers. They try things first and make a name for themselves. Others prefer to follow later and learn from the early adopters' mistakes. The messages we put forward, the language we use and the support we offer needs to look different for these two different groups so we can demonstrate we understand their aspirations.

As you get into it you will quickly realise you can sub-segment for ever. Let's imagine one of your key customer groups are schools. You can firstly segment them as senior schools and junior schools. The senior schools can then be broken down further into private or state schools. The state schools can be broken down further into free schools, academies and state maintained schools. Academies can be broken down further into those that are part of a large national or international group of academies or those that are part of a local trust, as they will have differing needs.

You can quickly come up with so many segments it is completely unmanageable and unproductive as the point of segmentation is to do something unique and meaningful for different segments.

Activity

Write down five meaningful customer segments for the market in which you operate

---

Once you have identified some important segments it is still necessary to analyse them to determine priorities as some of these segments will help you to achieve your objectives more readily than others. If we are saying each segments needs something different doing then prioritising the time you spend is very important.

I assess the segments identified using a set of simple criteria. I score each segment out of five against the following criteria:

Accessibility – you may have identified a great segment, but if you can't identify or get your message in front of the key decision makers then the segment becomes much less attractive. Take for example my friend who is looking for landlords with a social conscience – that is great, but how on earth does he identify them and get his message in front of them?

Size – typically the larger the segment the more room there is for you to expand in that segment.

Growth of segment – this isn't whether you are growing, but whether the segment as a whole is growing or shrinking. Are there likely to be more or less of that type of customer in the future?

Profitability – this may not be the final decision making criteria but it is important to know as it enables you to manage your portfolio and balance loss leading initiatives and social causes with segments that will generate a return.

Fit with your strengths – some segments naturally fit better with your history, experience and values than other segments. Those with a strong fit are likely to be the ones that you have most success with.

Relative strength of the competition – segments with less competition are obviously more attractive than those with established strong competitors.

Activity

Score the five segments you identified against these criteria

egment	Accessibility	Size	Growth	Profit	Fit	Competition	TOTAL

KNOWING YOUR CUSTOMERS

Once you have identified the key segments to work with you still need to understand them better so you know their needs and focus what you are doing around them. There are a number of ways of doing this. This list below is in no way exhaustive but is here just to give some tips and things to think about when finding out more about your customers. It is also important to take a proportionate approach to understanding your customers. If you are looking to spend £10million of your reserves based on your understanding of the market then a thorough and robust approach is needed. For activities with less risk, less time and cost should be taken.

Ask them – that's right, ask them what is important to them. This can take different forms; surveys, focus groups, one to one interviews and meetings. A few points to consider and think about: are the views of the customer you are speaking with representative? Are you asking questions that help you to understand their values? By that I mean I could be sent a survey asking if I'd like a new ice cream parlour in my village. I'd say yes! However that is very different to understanding how often I'd go in there and how much I'd be likely to spend. Surveys can sometime be dangerous as we jump to conclusions based on surface level questions and answers that don't probe deep enough. An academic research technique is called laddering. In essence this is asking why five times. They reckon if you ask why five times you move from surface level answers through to underlying values that can be used to determine likely behaviour.

View trends – industry reports can be used to look at customer behaviour on a large scale.

Study the competition – the good competitors out there probably understand your customer segments pretty well. Looking at 'what' they are doing and 'why' can help you to understand the customers as well.

Activity

What do you know about your key customer segments? Can you answer the following questions

What are their needs?

How are you going to help solve a problem for them?

How much do they currently buy?

How much do they pay?

Are they currently in contractual agreements?

How many customers are there in the segment?

How much of the market do you expect to win?

What are the 'winning themes' for that segment?

6.

THE COMPETITIVE ENVIRONMENT

The next area of analysis to consider is the competitive environment in which you operate. Unfortunately there are other forces at play which are influencing the customer segments you have identified and understanding these forces and developing strategies to counteract them is very important.

I think this is one of the most under developed areas of capability in the public sector and therefore represents an area of risk. If we make decisions without understanding these competitive forces our estimates and predications could turn out to be wildly inaccurate.

The starting point for understanding the competitive environment is not to look at your direct competitors, but to look first of all at the nature of the competition as it comes in many other forms than just direct competitors.

Budget level competition – If I have £1000 I could spend it on going on holiday or a new computer. Two completely different things, but if they are vying for the same pot of money they are still in competition with each other. This form of competition is often high if the services we are selling are discretionary; the customer doesn't have to do them. In my world of consultancy this is often the case. Frequently the clients are very price sensitive and spending on consultancy support means not spending on something else. When this is a form of competition we have to think about how we position ourselves to counteract it. Typically this would involve talking about value or return on investment or creating a desire to have the particular product or service you are selling.

Generic competition – this is a different way of meeting the same end goals. It isn't direct competition as it is doing something very differently, however the same end goals are being met by whichever approach. A form of this competition for me is e-learning. It is a very different approach to delivering the same outcome: learning. If this is a key form of competition in your market, again you need to consider what you can do to counteract it. For the training I do this comes down to two main choices: promoting the value of face to face training and the benefits that come with it or indeed also creating e-learning training so I compete in both markets.

Brand competition – this is the direct competition we often think about; someone else doing the same thing as us; Tesco or Sainsbury's. Don't be confused by the word brand, it isn't to do with how strong a brand is, it purely looks at the fact others are doing the same thing as us. This is almost always going to be a form of competition and increasingly it is going to come from other public sector organisations like yours doing the same thing as you. We will examine this in more detail later in the chapter.

Internal substitution – this is DIY competition, people doing for themselves. This is often a form of the competition for income generation opportunities that involve selling services to other public sector organisations. The competition comes from their internal departments. How can you persuade them to use you rather than to do it themselves? Where this is a key form of competition we have to again think about how to best position ourselves to counteract it.

When analysing the market, a question you should always be asking is 'what are the implications for me?' We need to think about how we position ourselves in response to the competitive forces at play. Positioning involves many things such as what we communicate to customers, our strategies for marketing and pricing.

Activity

Complete the table below to think through how these different types of competition affect the markets you operate in and what you can do to counteract them.

	How does this affect my market?	What can I do to counteract this competitive force?
Budget Level		
Generic		
Brand		
Internal Substitution		

Another useful model for examining the competitive forces is Porter's Five Forces. This model introduces a few areas that can impact on our competitiveness.

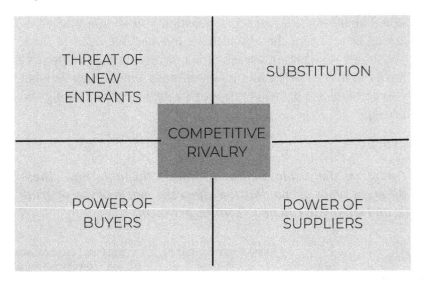

Competitive rivalry is pretty much the same as brand competition from the previous model, however the other four forces introduce something new.

Threat of new entrants – is there a threat that new providers will enter your market? This threat is typically high if there are low fixed costs associated with starting and no other real barriers to entry. In my world of consultancy this is a reality. There is nothing to stop existing consultancies entering the market or indeed new one man band outfits setting up. The challenge again is to think of what can be done to counter act the competition. For us it is about investing in the relationships with key clients.

Threat of substitution – is there a threat that a new way of doing things will come along that will make your way redundant?

Power of buyers – buyers are typically powerful when there are not many of them and many suppliers rely on them. When buyers are powerful they are able to exert pressure on suppliers to reduce cost or speed up delivery, both of which can have large consequences on the competitiveness of the supplying organisation.

Power of suppliers – suppliers are powerful when there are not many of them and they are relied upon for important goods or services. When suppliers are powerful they can again exert a pressure on us that can have a large impact on our ability to keep our customers happy. As an aside I think the public sector is pretty good at making our suppliers more powerful than they need to be. We do this by entering into framework agreements that artificially reduces the number of suppliers in the market thereby making each one more powerful. I know there are good reasons for this, particularly around the efficiency of the procurement process, however one of the unintended consequences is it actually increases their power. I've seen some research studies that suggest the cost of goods and services bought through some of the large national framework agreements is actually greater than if you went to the same organisations independently –why? Because they are actually more powerful within the framework than outside of it!

These five forces are deemed to be high if the following criteria are met:

Rivalry amongst existing firms

- Competitor balance
- Industry growth rate

- High fixed costs
- High exit barriers
- Low differentiation

Threat of new entrants

- Economies of scale
- Experience is key
- Access to supply or distribution channels
- Expected retaliation
- Legislation or government action
- Differentiation

Threat of substitute products

- The price / performance ratio

The power of suppliers

- Concentrated suppliers
- High switching costs
- Supplier competition threat

The power of buyers

- Concentrated buyers
- Low switching costs
- Buyer competition threat

Activity

How do these five forces affect your market and what can you do about it?

DIRECT COMPETITORS

Whatever the nature of the competitive forces in your market, there will always be an element of direct competition from others providing the same services as you. In some markets this will take the form of many small providers, in other markets there will be a few key competitors. When there are some major competitors it is very important to do what you can to understand them. By understanding their strengths and weaknesses you are able to develop strategies to maximise your strengths and focus on the needs of the customers in a way that they can't.

The following competitor swot analysis is a really useful tool to work through when examining your direct competitors. It works through the main aspects of an organisation and enables you to compare yourself against them. Finding the information needed about your competitors so you can answer the questions sometimes requires creative research. Possible sources for this include your customers, information from companies house, industry reports, staff who perhaps used to work for them and the competitor's own website.

As you will see from the table, some of the elements are more important than others. For instance, if you are providing a consultancy or advice service your competitor's financial standing and access to credit is unlikely to matter that much. If on the other hand you are creating a property development company then this becomes much more important.

Activity

Complete the Competitor SWOT on the next page for an important competitor in your market

	Performance					Importance		
	Major Strengths	Minor Strength	Neutral	Minor Weakness	Major Weakness	Hi	Med	Low
Marketing								
Company reputation								
Market share								
Customer satisfaction								
Customer retention								
Product quality								
Service quality								
Prricing effectiveness								
Distribution effectiveness								
Promotion effectiveness								
Sales force effectiveness								
Innovation effectiveness								
Geographical coverage								
Finance								
Cost or availability of capital								
Cash flow								
Financial stability								
Manufacturing								
Facilities								
Economices of scale								
Capacity								
Able, dedicated workforce								
Ability to produce on time								
Technical skills								
Organisation								
Visionary, capable leadership								
Dedicated employees								
Entrapreneurial orientation								
Flexible or responsive								

COMMERCIAL GOV

7.

POSITIONING

Once you have analysed the customer segments and the competitive environment those segments exist in, the next task is to then decide where in the market you are positioning yourself. There are a number of aspects to this; particularly pricing and branding, both of which we will look at in more detail shortly. However before getting into the specifics, the starting point is to think about where in the mind's eye of your customers you want to be positioned.

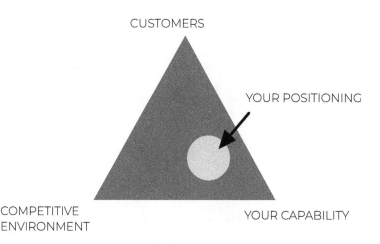

A good way of thinking about this is to look at the car market. Car models are specifically aimed at particular places in the market. Some are aspirational and desirable; others are low cost and practical with an increasing number of combinations. You have to combine your knowledge of the needs of the customer segments, the competitive environment and your strengths and weaknesses to determine the right position for you. There is no point having an aspiration to be the elite luxury brand if your customers don't want that and you don't have the capability to be that provider.

Activity

> *If you were to liken your product or service to a car, what make and model would it be and why?*

PRICE

Price does more to position a product than pretty much anything else. The impact price has varies considerably from market to market. Some markets are incredibly price sensitive whilst in others price conveys quality and value.

The starting point for pricing is to firstly understand your costs. Your costs provide the bottom of the pricing envelope. This is obviously important as if your price is less than your cost you will be losing money, which isn't very commercially astute! However understanding the true costs of the service is often one of the biggest challenges I come across in public sector organisations. This is because the part that is being commercialised is part of a bigger area that the budget is set against. This can make it very difficult to work out what the true cost is of delivering the service.

For a fair number of my clients the start of their commercial development journey has been to get a proper grip on their costs and then to change their existing fees and charges in line with the true cost of delivering those services.

Another issue with working out costs is overhead apportionment. How much of the corporate overhead is it right for the traded service to fund? An example I came across recently made for interesting reading:

I was working with a small district council to help them commercialise their trade waste service. In this particular authority overheads, or specifically IT overheads, were worked out on a per head basis. This particular unit had 55 staff, but only four of them were office based and there were five PCs in the office. It worked out they were paying £23,000 per year per PC for their IT! How on earth can they compete on an even playing field with their private sector competitors whilst carrying those sorts of costs? However, on the other hand, if they aren't paying that contribution towards the IT costs of the authority then someone else will have to pay a lot more.

There is no 'right answer' to this situation, but a clear strategy is needed. I've seen numerous different approaches to this:

- Incubator environments where traded services are released from some overheads for a period of time while they establish

- A requirement to pay full costs right from the word go so as not to buffer the service from financial realities

- A standalone set up where the service creates its own corporate functions and overheads

- A flexible approach to overhead apportionment knowing some traded areas can cope with more than others

Whilst I don't think there is a right answer. I do believe the overall mind-set of the corporate centre should be one of looking for what is best in each individual case. The whole reason services are trading is to generate income to bring back into the organisation. Therefore a mind-set of 'how can we best support them to succeed' is likely to deliver much greater results than sticking hard and fast to policies and procedures that work for some and don't for others.

An example of a flexible approach that is common to many local authorities can be seen by looking at Building Control. Building Control is an area that isn't allowed to make a profit, yet is probably one of the easiest parts of a local authority to commercialise. This has led many local authorities to a 'creative approach to overhead apportionment'! Whether this is right or wrong isn't the issue, it demonstrates the flexibility of thought that is required to succeed commercially.

When thinking about cost it is important to consider all of the costs involved in delivering the service or developing and selling the product. This includes all of the capital and revenue costs associated with the service. For high cost and therefore riskier investments an idea of return is also important and therefore financial management appraisals such as Net Present Value (NPV) and Internal Rate of Return (IRR) will be useful.

There also needs to be a view on what is the goal. This links back to the vision and objectives but also needs to be gauged in financial terms. Is profit the goal or is a contribution that wouldn't have existed before enough?

If cost is the bottom of the pricing envelope then the price elasticity of the market is the top of the envelope.

This means the sensitivity of the market to changes in price. For instance if I was selling the top of the range Rolls Royce and a new model came out that was £30,000 more than the last model then I would argue that it wouldn't affect sales as people just have to have it and £30,000 doesn't mean much to the people that would buy it. On the other hand if I was selling Mars Bars and I increased the price by 30p then I reckon sales would drop dramatically and everyone would buy another chocolate bar instead.

The reality is that often the top of the envelope, the sensitivity of the market to price, is only just above, or even sometimes below our costs and the only pricing decision to be made is how to keep costs as low as possible to keep them in line with market expectations!

If there is a pricing choice to be made then there are a number of common approaches to this:

Mark-up pricing – If it costs me £100 to deliver the service I will mark it up by 10% and charge £110. In my experience this is the favoured method for public sector accountants as it is easy and makes sense.

Target Return pricing – this looks longer term over an investment. For instance a city council I work with is developing commercially through an 'invest to save' mentality. They are open to pretty much any commercial venture if over a three year period the venture will make at least a 15% return. From this return, prices are then calculated.

Both of these approaches miss out on two important areas that are covered in market pricing.

Market pricing – this approach looks at what others are charging, what customers expect and tries to understand the psychological impact of pricing. For instance we've recently undertaken some work with some of the big banks. We quickly found that to be taken seriously we had to triple our day rate. Price said a lot about quality in that market and therefore we *had to respond.*

Activity

Have a look at the grid below that identifies nine different pricing strategies based on price and quality. Where on the grid would you position your product or service?

PRICE

	LOW	MEDIUM	HIGH
HIGH	SUPER VALUE STRATEGY	HIGH VALUE STRATEGY	PREMIUM STRATEGY
	GOOD VALUE STRATEGY	MEDIUM VALUE STRATEGY	OVERCHARGING STRATEGY
LOW	ECONOMY STRATEGY	FALSE ECONOMY STRATEGY	RIP OFF STRATEGY

QUALITY

I've asked thousands of public sector workers this question and only a tiny percentage would position it in a way so a higher price is charged than the level of quality provided. This is admirable and shows the values that underpin our public sector. These values have the potential to form part of a compelling competitive offer as we will explore when looking at branding. However it should also raise a warning note. A mind set I come across very frequently is; 'a desire to deliver a gold standard but only charge a bronze price'. This isn't commercially astute and will not result in objectives being hit which is, after all, the only reason that commercial development is happening at all.

8.

BRAND

I believe it is theoretically possible for the public sector to have as strong if not stronger brands than the big private sector brands.

This is a grand statement. I've yet to see it happen, other than the national NHS brand, but I will explain why I think it is possible and how I believe public sector organisations can use who they are and what they stand for to create a competitive advantage.

The starting place is to understand what a brand is. It is one of those words we hear all of the time but people mean different things by it. A definition of a brand that I think works is that it is a promise. It's a promise that we will get certain things with a certain level of service. The strength of that promise is either added to or taken away from through every interaction we have with the brand.

Now it is also important to mention at this point that people aren't always logical and rational and the way they relate to brands isn't always logical and rational. Take Apple geeks (I apologize if I am insulting you)! There is nothing logical or rational about queuing through the night to get the new iPhone on the first day it's released when you can get it through the post a few days later. Yet people do it because of the emotional engagement people have with brands.

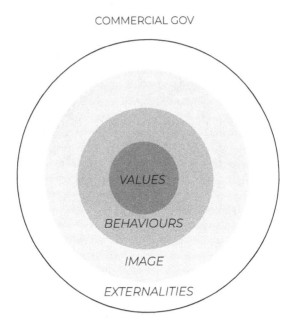

The Brand Power Wheel suggests the key components of a brand. At the centre of it are the values of the brand and the organisation. The model says that the job of the brand is to convey the values and that when the other areas; behaviours, image and externalities, are in alignment with the values and each other, then the brand is more powerful.

For instance, say there was a big telecoms provider who had excellent customer service as one of their values but when you called them you were left on hold for ages, when your call was eventually answered the operative was decidedly unhelpful, you got passed from pillar to post and eventually cut off. Those behaviours wouldn't be in alignment with the values and would therefore decrease the power of the brand.

Imagine a hi-tech Silicon Valley start-up as the demonstration of the 'image' part of this model. Lets say one of their values is that they are cutting edge. Now imagine a staff member insisted on using Comic Sans as the font in their email (a little pet hate of mine). I'd argue that wouldn't be in alignment with the values and would therefore detract from the power of the brand. You get the idea.

Now think back to that grand statement that I made. People are engaged with a brand when they see an alignment between their values; what's important to them, and the values they see the brand stand for. That is why communicating the values is so important. That is why Apple's brand is so strong. People want to be associated with the values they perceive Apple stands for. The values of public sector organisations are inherently good. Why wouldn't people want to be associated with them? Why wouldn't people want alignment with an organisation that stands for good public service, thriving communities and economic prosperity for the area? That is why I believe it is possible to create really strong public sector brands, because the values that underpin the brands are good, in fact often better than the values that underpin many of the big brands.

I do realise that there are many problems with this and barriers to achieving this. Firstly the average person's perception of the values of the public sector is not necessarily the reality. If you ask an average person what a council stands for you would quite likely get words like 'bureaucratic' and 'ponderous' in amongst other more complimentary terms. The nature of many public sector organisations also makes it difficult to manage and police. For instance you could be selling a great leisure service, but if my bins aren't collected on time I could get annoyed with the local authority and that would tarnish everything associated with it. Over recent years the brand of many parts of the public sector has also arguably been tarnished by some of central government's policies and rhetoric, which doesn't help.

However, given all of that, I still believe it is possible to develop strong brands. The challenge is how to better communicate the values as they are inherently good!

Now I've been told, although I haven't been able to corroborate this, that there are now more internal branding agencies in London than external ones. That means there are more focusing on the link between staff and the values of the organisation than there are on focusing on design, logos corporate identity etc. Now I don't know for sure if this is true. However what is true is there is now a much greater emphasis on internal branding than there used to be, and for a clear reason. Research clearly shows that engaged staff = engaged customers. If we want to strengthen our brands the effort really starts with our staff.

A friend of mine worked for Mini when they were taken over by BMW. When the takeover first occurred he said the BMW people came and 'they weren't like normal people'! He said that he thought if you cut them their blood would be black, white and blue as they were so obsessed with BMW. He then went on to say that they were now trying to brainwash the Mini staff with the BMW way. In branding language this is called 'living the brand'. Helping staff understand what the values look like in action in every part of their role and understanding and buying into the importance of that.

Now many years later it is, by all accounts it has worked. He says if you meet Mini employees in the pub at the weekend you will never hear one of them say anything bad about BMW. They are proud to work for them and buy into the BMW way. These are engaged employees and this engagement overflows into a passion for the company so much so that any employee, whether they are on the manufacturing line or in the showroom, is a sales person for the company.

I believe this demonstrates the main difference between the big brands and the public sector. The big brands have invested heavily in the hearts and minds of their staff. Some public sector organisations are now having value based competencies, which his great, but I've yet to come across the same focused effort.

WHAT BRAND?

A common question I get asked is whether everything should remain under the main organisation brand or whether new brands should be created. I'm not sure there is a simple answer to this or indeed a right answer. The big private sector companies don't all do the same thing which probably means there are alternative ways to the same end goal. For instance compare Virgin with Unilever. Virgin clearly brands everything pretty much the same way even though products vary greatly. Unilever on the other hand often has no link back to the parent company and follow a 'house of brands' approach.

The focus should always be on the end goal and a flexible approach should then be adopted that will make the objectives more likely to be achieved rather than a rigid one brand approach. However the service managers might not be the best ones to decide that and assumptions made should be clearly tested.

An example of this comes from a district council I've been working with. They have developed a flexible approach to branding for their commercial initiatives whilst still retaining control over the brand. They've developed a new brand that strongly links to the main local authority brand for some of the services to businesses that they offer such as trade waste, pest control and building control. For these services it is beneficial being linked to the council as the council is trusted, it's not going anywhere and they are not going to steal your money. However for other commercial areas, such as their municipal golf course, they have changed the branding quite substantially.

Golfers don't want to be associated with a local authority! By changing the signage and removing any indication that the course was linked to the council they were able to increase the usage (and therefore income) quite substantially.

The main reason for the development of commercial services in the public sector is to generate income. Therefore the question to ask is 'what brand is going to achieve that most successfully?' Sometimes the answer will be the existing corporate brand and sometimes it won't be. When the corporate brand isn't used that might mean that the organisation has to sacrifice taking the credit for the success of the venture in return for generating greater profits, which ultimately is the objective.

Developing new brand names and identities is an art in itself. There are many agencies that will do this for you. Don't just use graphic designers though. They produce great looking logos but without necessarily understanding the customers you are looking to engage with. Always test ideas and designs with customers and generally keeping it simple is a good idea.

9.

INVESTMENTS

FINANCIAL INVESTMENTS

All public sector organisations will have a policy for the way they appraise capital investments. It is very important to apply the same thinking to investments required to develop commercially or indeed to invest in a commercial opportunity.

I've have frequently comes across situations where an investment opportunity has been identified. The costs and the likely return have been identified and then the financial analysis has stopped there. To effectively appraise an investment opportunity it has to be compared to something else as there are always options, even if that option is just receiving interest from the bank. Just looking for other opportunities to use as comparison often identifies greater opportunities that give a better return, but perhaps look too big and scary to begin with.

It is also vital that the lifetime costs of investments are factoring into the appraisal. I often come across examples where external funding has been found for regeneration initiatives which have a positive impact on the community and sometimes create yield for the local authority. However, what hasn't been taken into account is the operational cost of looking after the asset into the future.

IMPACT OF THE PUBLIC WORKS LOANS BOARD REVIEW

The consultation on changing the borrowing rules through the Public Works Loan Board (PWLB) have been much anticipated by local government as it has potentially wide-reaching impacts on the options local authorities have for making investments and generating yield for offsetting budget cuts.

As in all markets, there has been a full range of investment strategies demonstrated by local government. However, borrowing to generate yield to some degree or another has become common place and has increasingly become an important part of the commercial development of local authorities with the income generated also becoming vital to offset budget cuts.

The publication of the new PWLB rules and guidance on 25th November 2020 identifies what is now allowable and possible. This section looks at the rules and guidance to look at what options are still open to local authorities and how borrowing from the PWLB can still be part of their commercial development.

The New Guidance

The new guidance seems to be looking to stop local authorities from borrowing if the intention of the borrowing is primarily for the generation of yield. Capital spending plans will have to be submitted in advance, and if a local authority intends to buy commercial assets primarily for yield (even using reserves) then they will be prevented from taking any PWLB borrowing in that financial year. This will stop Finance Directors from reprofiling the capital programme so that borrowing is only used on allowed projects, with internal borrowing used for commercial activities.

Each local authority that wishes to borrow from the PWLB will in future have to submit a high-level description of their capital spending and financing plans for the following three years, including their expected use of the PWLB. Local authorities will be able to revise these plans in-year as required.

The Section 151 Officer or equivalent will have to provide an assurance that the local authority is not borrowing in advance of need and does not intend to buy investment assets primarily for yield.

When applying for a new loan, the local authority will be required to confirm that the plans they have most recently submitted remain current and that the assurance that they do not intend to buy investment assets primarily for yield remains valid.

What Borrowing is Authorised?

The guidance sets out categories of borrowing that are authorised. These include:

• Service spending

• Housing

• Regeneration

• Preventative

• Treasury Management

Individual projects and schemes may have characteristics of several different categories of course. In these cases, the Section 151 Officer or equivalent of the authority will need to use their professional judgement to assess the main objective of the investment and consider which category is the best fit.

What will be the Result?

The nature and type of local authority investments will definitely change. Out of area acquisitions will be very hard to justify within the new guidance. However, the categories of authorised borrowing are broad enough to allow different interpretations through which arise different possibilities for commercial investment.

Housing

The Housing category is activity normally captured in the HRA and General Fund housing sections of the COR, or housing delivered through a local authority housing company. This does provide scope on the face of it, for continuation of housing schemes, including through LA owned companies, and does not appear to restrict the borrowing to social or affordable housing.

Regeneration

Regeneration projects are described in the guidance as having characteristics that fall into one of four areas:

1. the project is addressing an economic or social market failure by providing services, facilities, or other amenities that are of value to local people and would not otherwise be provided by the private sector.

2. the local authority is making a significant investment in the asset beyond the purchase price: developing the assets to improve them and/or change their use, or otherwise making a significant financial investment.

3. the project involves or generates significant additional activity that would not otherwise happen without the local authority's intervention, creating jobs and/or social or economic value.

4. while some parts of the project may generate rental income, these rents are recycled within the project or applied to related regeneration projects, rather than being applied to wider services.

These characteristics are relatively broad and potentially leave room for flexibility in project scope for commercial initiatives. For instance, we are currently working on commercial projects with a couple of local authorities that are about addressing market failure. However, by addressing the market failure the local authority will not only be positioned to provide a better service for residents but will also generate income and savings in the process.

The central point of the guidance is what the investment is primarily for, given that many projects will straddle the boundaries of the categories. If local authorities have any projects that are primarily for yield, then borrowing is simply not available to them.

However, that does not prevent local authorities from borrowing for projects that are primarily for other purposes, which also happen to generate a financial yield.

For authorities that wish to continue to generate commercial income in order to protect services, the challenge will be finding projects that deliver much more than financial yield, such that they cannot be accused of investing in projects primarily for yield. Any yield in any such projects will have to be secondary to another prime purpose.

To achieve this a wide definition of what 'being commercial' will be needed. Local authorities will need to get better at understanding the link between social impact and commercial return and will need to think about how they can become a more integral 'part of the infrastructure' of their communities and particularly regeneration initiatives.

What other opportunities are there?

There are still other ways for local authorities to invest in commercial property.

It should be possible to ring-fence rents from an existing 'yield' project, recycling them either within the project, or applying them to other similar projects with related or similar project outcomes.

The requirement on the S151 Officer set out in the guidance is to provide an assurance that the local authority is not borrowing in advance of need and does not intend to buy investment assets primarily for yield. It does not ask you to provide assurance that you are not investing in assets primarily for yield.

Where you already have yield based assets, you could ring-fence some of that existing revenue income to invest on that asset, or other yield bearing assets, to improve investment performance and yields.

This might be a case of looking at your existing 'legacy' property portfolio and spotting opportunities where an injection of investment could generate greater yields.

Because the guidance is framed around borrowing to buy and not borrowing to invest, there appears to be no restriction on borrowing to build new yield-bearing investments on existing local authority land.

Another option to consider might be buying 'yield' projects where you intend to inject further investment beyond the initial purchase price. This might be through refurbishing or re-purposing the acquired asset. This appears to be a perfectly legitimate borrowing category.

The new guidance shows there are still opportunities to invest and to generate investment income. However, to achieve this requires local authorities to approach investment in a more rounded way, linking investment opportunities much more closely to the delivery of the corporate plan than many have before. The investment opportunities will take more work and more thinking through, however there are still opportunities within the new guidelines to generate yield through investment. Yield can't be the only or primary reason for the investment. This means that investments have the potential to generate much more than just yield if done well.

OTHER INVESTMENT OPPORTUNITIES

The type of institution that public sector bodies are means they are good investments. The rest of this chapter highlights one of many other potential investment routes. This route has led to:

the Marischal Square Development, Aberdeen, the New Bailey Development, Salford and the Stevenson Quarter in Newcastle to name a few. The local authorities typically pay rent of 60-65% of the ERV which means if they are able to fully occupy the space there is a large profit to be made.

Government Gilt yields are at historic lows meaning investors seeking to purchase alternative investments of similar quality with matching characteristics. Financial Institutions such as annuity providers are looking for stable, low risk, index-linked income.

There is market demand driven by the baby boomer generation who don't benefit from final salary pensions, but who have saved for retirement in pension schemes that provide a capital amount on retirement to invest in an annuity that will provide an income on retirement.

Annuity providers need to purchase assets which provide the type of income that matches their liabilities, plus provide a small margin to cover their costs & profit.

Public bodies and financially strong corporates have a financial strength that is attractive for this type of investment. Asset rich local authorities with strong balance sheets & strict financial control, provide counterparty risk akin to sovereign risk (underwritten by central government)

Deals are structured typically where the investor acquires the freehold or long leasehold of the asset with the public body / corporate taking a lease with annual RPI (capped & collared) uplifts.

Investors are typically pension and annuity providers – providing pension products and annuities for employees throughout the UK.

Investment Yields

Investment yields are driven by three key factors:

- Strength of the covenant and underlying income steam - often the head tenant sub-lets the accommodation and can make a large profit rent (this is also a comfort for the investors).

- Length of the income strip - the longer the better but there is investor appetite from 20 years upwards (sweet spot 35-50 years)

- Rental uplift mechanism – annual RPI is preferred but with a cap & collar in place to create a band within which this can operate (usually 0-4%).

- Quantum of 'profit rent' received by Council - difference

between the tenant lease annual rent and that to which the Council is committing on the income-strip lease

Investment Suitability

- Any type of property is potentially suitable

- The investor is more focused on the financial strength of the covenant and structure of the lease, rather than the asset.

- Deals have been agreed on offices; retail units; student accommodation; social housing; infrastructure; hotels & car parks

- Factors to consider:

  - Sector (dynamics, defensibility, cyclicality etc.)
  - Asset quality (age, construction)
  - Location (current use & development potential)
  - Covenant strength of tenant
  - Lease (indexed, FRI, break clauses etc.)
- Council's preference = single let, secure assets; not multi-let

Summary of Key Terms

Asset: good location, good asset quality, good covenant

Counterparty: Public bodies and financially strong corporates

Funder: Institutional Investor (pension & annuity providers)

Cash flow: stable, low risk, index-linked income

Profit Rent: 20-25%

Yield: 3.0 to 3.5% for a 35-yr term (depending on strength of the underlined asset, the covenant of each local authority, and also the indexation)

Term: 35-50 years

Quantum: £20-80 million

Lease: Full Repairing & Insuring

Cap & Collar: 0-4% reviewed annually & RPI or CPI linked

10.

COMMERCIAL BUSINESS CASES

A business case provides the justification for initiating a project or task. It evaluates the benefit, cost and risk of alternative options and provides a rationale for investing in a preferred solution. As a management tool, it is developed incrementally over time as the proposal matures, with additional detail added with each iteration. It is essential to pass the business case through the appropriate gateways for approval at each stage so that options can be effectively appraised to enable robust decision-making and stakeholder buy-in.

This is common to public sector managers, however a good commercial business case needs to ask different questions to standard service business cases to effectively evaluate the benefit, cost and risk of alternative commercial options.

An effective commercial business case must also be proportionate. The whole point of operating commercially is to deliver a return. If producing the business case takes so long, or indeed is so complex we need external support to pull it together, then to some degree it defeats the whole point of the business case.

A good commercial business case must also help decision makers evaluate one investment opportunity against another, even if they are very different. Resources are finite including the time and capacity of our people to implement new ideas. Therefore one opportunity must be evaluated against other ones so the overall portfolio of commercial growth is balanced, focused, diverse and built around the initiatives that will give the best return.

I am a big fan of a staged approach to business cases. Stage one is a simple business case template that gets managers to think in the right way, answer key questions and present options against common criteria. We help many public sector organisations turn the commercial framework on page 31 into a stage one business case template. This model ensures key commercial questions are thought about and answered in the development of the case. This includes areas such as: customer segmentation, competitor analysis, positioning, sales forecasting and pricing. These areas are not common to traditional public sector business cases but need to be looked at to accurately evaluate the benefit, cost and risk of commercial opportunities.

If the risk is high and the level of investment required is also high then a further more detailed business should also be required. A common and effective model for this is the Office of Government Commerce Five Case Model for Business Cases. The "Five Case Model" is the best practice standard recommended by

HM Treasury for use in central government departments, other government bodies and by all those with responsibility for deciding how public money should best be spent.

The five cases in support of a proposal for a commercial opportunity must demonstrate they have thought in detail about the following questions:

The strategic case - "What we are doing and why?"

The economic case - "Available options and the extent to which they provide value for money?"

The commercial case - "How will the project or programme be delivered?"

The financial case - "How much it will cost, and how it will be funded?"

The management case - "How will delivery of the programme/project be planned, monitored and overseen to evaluate and ensure its success?"

The main difference between this detailed stage and the stage 1 business case is the level of detail in the economic and financial case and the delivery plan in the management case. We won't go into the detail required, but guidance can be found online for the five case model. However, the table below describes the differences between the economic and financial cases and the type of type of analyses required:

Factor	Economic Appraisals	Financial Appraisals
Focus	VFM – net present value/net present cost (NPV/NPC).	Affordability – cash flow
Coverage	Wide coverage – Government and society	Relevant organisation(s)
Relevant standards	HM Treasury Green Book rules[1] -Real discount rate which changes after year 30	Organisational accounting rules and standing orders.
Analysis	- Constant (real) prices; - Includes opportunity cost; - Includes indirect and attributable costs – costs of others; - Includes all quantifiable costs, benefits and risks; - Excludes all Exchequer transfer'payments – for example, VAT; - Excludes general inflation; sunk costs, depreciation and capital charges.	- Current (nominal) prices; - Benefits – cash releasing only; - Includes transfer payments (for example, VAT); - Includes inflation; depreciation and capital charges.

11.

STAKEHOLDERS

The success or failure of any project is pretty much always down to people! Commercial projects are no different at all. There are a wide number of internal and external stakeholders that must be navigated through to successfully develop, launch and run commercial initiatives. These stakeholders include senior managers, elected members, the public, the press, staff working on the project and the wide variety of different existing and potential customers.

The tools and models involved in developing commercially can sometimes make it seem like it is all about rational thought and almost scientific like disciplines. The truth is a million miles away from that. It is people and the relationships we build with them that matters most and therefore this must be an area that we focus our time and attention on.

The starting place is good old fashioned stakeholder analysis. Who are your main stakeholders, the ones that are likely to have an impact on the development of your ideas and the implementation of them? How much power do they have over your likely success and how interested are they in it?

Activity

> **List the stakeholders and rate them on their power and interest**

I like to develop socio-grams to depict this information as this enables you to plot the relationships between the stakeholders. The size of the circle depicts the power of the stakeholder and the distance from you the interest that they have.

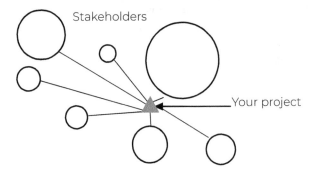

Where possible think of individuals not groups as it is individuals we develop relationships with and can ultimately influence. If you are a school looking to develop commercially, one of your stakeholder groups would be the parents. There isn't one representative parent who speaks for and influences the rest so you would treat parents as a group. However, if HR is a stakeholder, who in HR is the real influencer? Who really makes the decisions because that is the person you need to develop a relationship with.

To be 'commercially aware' is to focus on the relationships that really matter and to do something about them. This means a key skill of a commercial manager is to know how to influence others. This is very different to manipulation; where you try to get others to do things they don't want to do. Influencing is about building win win relationships. These stakeholders could be internal or external to your organisation. Very often the skill is actually about how to navigate the internal politics of your organisation to get things done. Organisational awareness and nowse is needed!

Cialdidi is probably the most authoritative author on influencing. He has identified six factors of influence which are described below. As you read about them think about the stakeholders who have power over your commercial objectives. How could you apply some or all of the methods of influencing to your relationship with them?

1 RECIPROCATION

When someone gives you something of perceived value you immediately respond with the desire to give something back.

For example - every Christmas people buy gifts and send cards to people for whom they care little. Why? Because they will be receiving something from them as well – there is a feeling of obligation. A recent study reports that a psychology professor sent cards to lots of people he didn't know with his address – the next year; he received cards back from over 70% of these strangers.

Another example - offering a mint with the bill in a restaurant increases the size of tip.

Amway, the direct sales organisation, allows you to try the products for free; using them creates a feeling of obligation to purchase them.

Each person carries a "favour bank" – think of child care. A friend takes the kids to school today and you immediately feel the obligation to repay.

People dislike being in this position of obligation or "owing": ask yourself how do you feel when you are in this situation?

What makes this rule so strong is not just the obligation to repay, but also there appears to be a feeling of obligation to receive – i.e. it is rude to refuse when somebody offers you something. This makes the law very easy to apply.

The rule also seems to be disproportionate – give a little and get a lot back.

Activity

How can you support the agendas of your key stakeholders, both internal and external ones, knowing that if you do they are more likely to help you with your commercial agenda in return?

---

2 COMMITMENT AND CONSISTENCY

When an individual announces that he/she is taking a position on any issue or point of view, they will tend to strongly defend that position, regardless of its accuracy and even in the face of overwhelming evidence to the contrary.

When someone you believe in or respect expects you to perform a task or achieve results, you will tend to fulfil this expectation whether positive or negative.

This is linked to consistency – we want to conform to people's expectations of us.

"Okay you think I am a bad boy – I'll be naughty"

Or you create the expectation that they will make a decision at the end of the meeting – they then feel that they need to comply.

Activity

How does this apply to your stakeholders? Are you able to create a positive expectation of them?

3 SOCIAL PROOF

This is called different things at different stages of our lives. When we are kids at school it is called peer pressure and when we are professionals in the workplace it's called 'best practice'. However it is fundamentally the same – "everyone else is doing it so should we"!

Most people tend to agree to proposals, or services that will be perceived as acceptable by the majority of other people or a majority of an individual's peer group.

85% of the population are conformists – they want to be accepted by the majority. So do not make your offer so exceptional that they will stand out – instead show how they fit in more!

10% are termed contrarian conformists. They want to be different from the majority but they then form their own group of people who want to be different! Punks, Goths, Golfers!

Broadcasters use laughter tracks – everybody hates them but testing indicates that shows, with laugh tracks are always rated as funnier. Even though we know the laughter is fake, our click-whirr takes over.

And these are not new – in Italy in the early nineteenth century there were professional 'claqueurs' – people who were paid to applaud when a particular person came on stage – they had tariffs ranging from wild enthusiasm through to gentle applause.

Activity

How are you able to use social proof to influence your stakeholders?

4 FAMILIARITY AND LIKING

We tend to prefer goods, services and ideas that are promoted by people or groups we find likable or respect.

Unfortunately we are all shallow! Study after study shows that people prefer attractive people – not just physically; they also perceive them as kinder, more intelligent and even more honest. They get lighter fines in court – even lighter jail sentences.

Therefore try to look as attractive as possible! This isn't about being unfeasibly gorgeous but that you should attempt to look as acceptable and attractive as those you are seeking to influence.

Friends are people that we like – and perceive to be like us – so the more you match, the more successful you will be.

You may match on several levels:

- background
- values
- school
- nationality etc

and in the sense of rapport – physiology, tone, language etc.

It is about being 'one of us'. Next time you buy a car from a dealer, look and listen for attempts to influence based on the principle of familiarity and liking.

Flattery really works!

Activity

> *An uncomfortable but very valid question is 'what can you do to make your stakeholders like you more?*

5 AUTHORITY

People have power over other people to the degree that they are perceived as having greater authority,

Strength or expertise count as alternative forms of authority...

With expertise what goes through the persons mind is: *"You know so much about this. You will think that I am stupid if I do not do as you suggest."*

A famous case study

Imagine a university researcher asks you to help them with an experiment on the impact of punishment on reinforcing learning. To test it, he is going to ask a volunteer to study some word pairs. Then they will go into another room and have an electrode attached to them. You will then ask questions; each time the volunteer gets an answer wrong an electric shock is to be administered. The voltage is to be increased with each wrong answer. As you get to 50V, there are audible grunts. As you reach 130V you hear the subject screaming for you to stop. You complain to the researcher that the pain is so great that they cannot possibly get anymore right. But he insists that you carry on and what is more, if they don't answer you are to increase the voltage. The screams are never ending – agonising. Until they finally stop.

Would you carry on?

Psychologists predicted that about 1 person in a thousand would carry on to the end. In practice – 60% went the whole way. This is the Milgram experiment. Subjects even continued when the victim informed them of a serious heart condition.

So who were these people? On a battery of personality tests the group came out as Joe Average – there were no indications that they were any different from anyone else. Milgram's conclusion – the power of authority overrides our sense of right and wrong.

We believe that in most instances, following orders makes sense – 'they' know more than we do, 'they' know best.

In another, more comedic case a hospital patient was being treated for intense pain in their ear. A senior physician scribbled a prescription for drops to be administered to "R ear". A nurse administered the drops rectally! The patient made a complete recovery within a few days.

This made no sense but that's what the doctor had said so everyone played their part – nurse and patient.

A best-seller and winner of the National Book Award in America retyped and sent her manuscript under an assumed name of an unknown author to 22 reputable publishers. All rejected it as unsuitable for publication, including the book's publisher.

Activity

How can you leverage the authority you or others involved with you have and are there ways that you can give power to stakeholders as giving them power also influences them?

---

6 SCARCITY

When a person perceives that something they might want is limited in quantity, they believe that the value of what they might want is greater than if it were available in abundance.

At work never say that you are available any time and any place. Offer 20 minutes on Thursday. The immediate perception is that your time is important and valuable.

This works because not having access to something reduces our freedom of choice. Also generally the best things do go first.

Similarly if something is SECRET – e.g. only for our BEST clients, it will be more valued.

Activity

How does the principle of scarcity apply to the way you work with your stakeholders?

The reality is that often the most important and trickiest stakeholders are the internal ones. Organisational awareness is one of the emotional competencies identified by Daniel Goleman in his work on emotional intelligence. Knowing how to get things to work in your organisation is so important in turning a good idea into a reality.

12.

IMPLEMENTATION - SYSTEM, STRUCTURE AND PROCESS

Any strategy is only as good as your ability to implement it and it's exactly the same with a commercial strategy. We will look at implementation from three different perspectives which in my experience are three of the most important areas to consider when developing commercially. They are:

- System, structure and process

- People and Culture

- Marketing capability

SYSTEM, STRUCTURE AND PROCESS

A great model for starting to look at how to implement a commercial strategy is McKinsey's 7S Framework.

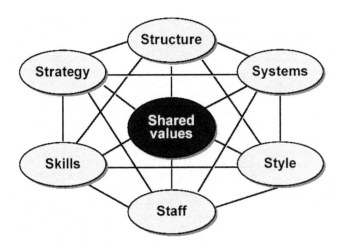

This model suggests that for things to be working well these different 'S's' have to be adding value to each other. The starting point for us is the Strategy 'S'. Imagine you are now in a position to implement a new commercial strategy, how are the other areas helping or hindering you from implementing the strategy?

Structure – Structure talks about the structure of the organisation but also the reporting lines and responsibility that the income generating unit has. Does it have the autonomy required to operate successfully? Are the senior staff above the unit understanding and supportive? Are there pressures to deliver the 'in-house service' as a priority over the income generating service?

Many years ago I was undertaking a Masters in Marketing where my dissertation looked at the commercial development of the public sector. I came across an interesting case study during this study that links to this area of structure. There was a training and consultancy service of a County Council that was trading with other organisations to generate income. The head of the unit was also the head of OD for the County Council. On interviewing this person it turned out that about 10% of their focus was on turning the unit into a commercial success. About 80% of their attention was on delivering the internal OD agenda and about 10% of their attention was on what they could do to become the next HR Director (they were very honest).

Their main competition came in the form of a locally based small consultancy that was run by someone who had worked in the public sector. 100% of their attention was focused on making that business a commercial success.

The managerial focus and ambition is strongly influenced by the structures we create and in turn impacts the likely success of an income generating unit.

Systems

The systems that we use to run and manage our businesses have such an impact on them and the success they have. Systems include: IT, HR, Health and Safety and decision making to name just a few. Do these systems add value and lead to success in the commercial entities we set up or do they create bureaucracy and slow decision making down?

The fact is that most of the systems we have are created for a large public sector organisation and the needs of a commercial unit may be very different. We need to find flexible approaches to balancing speed and rigour and a one size fits all approach to systems is unlikely to work.

Decision making is often where the biggest difference is seen between a public sector commercial entity and their private sector competition. The competition can make a key strategic decision almost immediately and get on and implement it. In the public sector those decisions typically take much longer as the governance structures in place are not designed for quick decision making. Later on we will look at different structures that can be used to speed up this process whilst maintaining strong governance and accountability of public money.

Style

The style of an organisation or the culture that exists has an enormous impact on commercial ventures. We will explore this in more detail in the next chapter. In general terms commercial entities need a culture that accepts risks, looks to learn from mistakes rather than avoid mistakes, and empowers staff to try things through the approach taken to recruitment, reward and promotion. This is different to the typical culture of a large traditional public sector organisation.

Staff

Are there the right staff, doing the right things in the right place with the right support and focus? Often commercial initiatives start by asking staff to do it as well as the day job. Is this the right way? Are there ways of spotting the areas in which additional staff investment will create better results?

Skills

Do the staff have the right skills needed to succeed? Are there places within the organisation they can go for specialist help in areas such as market analysis, marketing, finance and social media to name a few.

Activity

> *Spend some time auditing your organisation based on these 'S's'. Where are the strengths and where are the weaknesses when it comes to implementing new commercial strategies? What can be done in the areas that seem to be destroying value from the initiative?*

The following is adapted from Johnson and Scholes' *Exploring Corporate Strategy*. It analyses the value adding or destroying role the corporate parent can have over the business units that are part of it. I used this model when analysing traded services in my masters dissertation and have since used it on many occasions to look at the way the corporate centre adds or destroys value from its commercial initiatives:

VALUE ADDING ROLE

Efficiency / leverage

Can be created through scale advantages in the use of infrastructure, support services and other overhead items. Care has to be taken that by adding value through efficiency and leverage, value isn't destroyed by the increased bureaucracy it can create.

Expertise

Providing expertise not available in smaller units such as HR, financial services and ICT.

Investment

This can be vital in the early days of a new venture. Two key areas are competence building to develop the commercial competencies needed within the service and cash flow which can be a huge benefit over an equivalent private sector organisation.

Fostering Innovation

This could involve coaching, peer-led learning and the general management of the knowledge creation process. It also involves creating the right environment for new ideas to be tried.

Mitigating Risk

Risk is inevitable for smaller services, by being part of something bigger, the parent can mitigate risk.

Image / Networks

The 'brand' of the parent can add value when used properly. The networks of people from the corporate centre are also potentially very valuable. The challenge is to have a corporate system that captures these networks for use by the commercial services.

Collaboration / Coordination / Brokerage Standards / Performance Assessment

Encouraging partnerships between different areas of the organisation that might not otherwise work together.

Standards / Performance Assessment

Setting standards, monitoring performance and intervening to improve performance.

Acting in a Visionary Capacity

Providing clear strategic intent and an attractive challenge of the future can help to stimulate creativity and innovation in developing business-level strategy.

VALUE DESTROYING ROLE

Adding cost and creating a bureaucratic fog

Adding cost and delaying decision making that hinders market responsiveness. Delegated decision making is vital to ensure responsiveness.

Buffering businesses from financial realities

The corporate parent can buffer services from financial realities by providing a 'safety net' that means managers are not truly answerable for the performance of the services. These can mean hard decisions aren't made as the parent buffers the consequences of not making them.

Providing a focus for managerial ambition

Corporate hierarchies provide a focus for managerial ambition. This can result in a lack of time and attention spent on ensuring the service performs.

Creating the right relationship between the commercial initiative and the corporate body has an enormous impact on the likely success of the initiative and therefore the benefits that it brings back to the corporate body. My belief is that we should start with the end in mind; what benefits are we looking for and therefore what is the best way to set it up and make it relate to the corporate body? All too often commercial initiatives are hamstrung by having to follow the same corporate approach that all services are made to follow. This reduces effectiveness and limits the benefits that are realised, which ultimately is the only reason commercial discussions are being had in the public sector at the moment.

13.

IMPLEMENTATION - PEOPLE AND CULTURE

Culture is a real buzz word in the business world at the moment. However it is for good reason. Peter Drucker's famous quote: *'culture eats strategy for breakfast'* may seem like the sort of phrase you would hear David Brent saying in The Office. However it is completely true. No strategy will reach maturity if it isn't planted within a culture that is conducive to it growing. Therefore as we look to implement our commercial initiatives, we have to take notice of the culture we have, the culture we require and how we bridge the gap from one to another.

WHAT IS CULTURE?

Early on in my career I worked for a local authority that wasn't a happy place. It was going through a large change and there was a lot of internal politics and jostling for power. The result of this was a culture of negativity that spread like a cancer. Groups of staff couldn't have a normal conversation without talking about certain key issues. Everyone had an opinion, these opinions differed but the result was negativity, pessimism and ultimately depression.

I enjoyed work, was very ambitious and consciously decided to distance myself from these unhealthy dynamics. However, without realizing, it affected me badly. I never really joined in the negative talk, but the environment sapped the life out of me, took any joy out of the work and made me look for a quick exit! The culture of the workplace had affected me and I had become like everyone else without ever intending to.

The fact is we are influenced by other people. Realising this is important in understanding why we and our staff make the decisions we do and behave the way we behave. More important however, is learning how to control the impact influences have on us and our staff and how to develop a culture within our organisations that develop and are nurtured through generating positive influences.

WHAT INFLUENCES US?

We are influenced by others on a variety of levels. The highest level is the culture that exists in the communities we are part of. As culture changes it influences us. One example of this is the way elders in society are viewed and how this has changed over time. I'm not using this example to make a point about honouring our elders, although it could easily be used to do that, but merely to look at how changes in culture influence us and our behaviours.

When my parents were children they addressed other adults as 'Sir' or 'Madam'. When I was a child I addressed other adults as 'Mr Smith' or 'Mrs Jones'. My children address other adults by their Christian names, as do the vast majority of other children. The expectation society has on the way adults are addressed over these three generations has changed and the last three generations of my family has adapted to this change. My family has been influenced by culture changing and followed suit.

At a different level we are influenced by patterns and trends in culture. Fashion and hairstyles are good examples of this. When I was a teenager, a centre parting, long curtains and an undercut were all the style. I followed this style and have many embarrassing photos to remind me! Looking around today I can't see any young people with a haircut like that, probably just as well!

When I was a teenager, with my curtains and undercut, my Dad got a white Ford Sierra with a spoiler on the back. I thought it was the best car going and loved arriving at school or at friends' houses in it. Fast forward a few years and white became such an unpopular colour for a car that if you were buying a second hand car and had a choice between a white one and pretty much any other colour, the white one would have been considerably less expensive because the colour was so unpopular. Nowadays white cars are en vogue again and represent a large percentage of new car sales. As these trends and patterns change over time, we are influenced by them and follow suit.

The third level of culture we are influenced by is the culture of the groups that we belong to. This includes the organisations and the extended families we are part of. If you think about your family and compare it to other families you know, I'm sure you can pick out some pretty large cultural differences. This becomes particularly obvious when it comes to marriage and then is highlighted further when the first baby comes along and the cultures of parenting you were used to suddenly become so important even though you vowed as a child to never do the same to your kids!

We are influenced by culture. To understand how this impacts on us in the workplace we need to dig a bit deeper to understand how and why it influences us in the way that it does. Psychologists Tajfel and Turner demonstrated that we find our social identity from the groups that we are part of. They found we strongly favour people in the groups that we are in, even if those groups don't represent anything and people have just been randomly assigned to them. So just being part of a group, whether or not we like the others in the group, agree with what it stands for, or do anything in the group, creates an allegiance to it. This means that the groups we are part of, both formal and informal have a strong influencing affect over us.

The fourth level of cultural influence is the people you spend the most time with. Psychologist, Albert Bandura, showed that people learn by observing what others do. He found that we copy the behaviours of others. If the behaviour is good and positive then this can be a positive trait. If it is negative behaviour then the impact on us is also negative.

Cialdini built on this research to show that we actually look to others to see how to behave, especially in; ambiguous situations that we haven't encountered before and in crisis and when we perceive others to be experts. In his original experiment he had some accomplices stare upwards on a street pavement as if they were looking at something although there was actually nothing there! Other people quickly joined them and a large group formed and stayed there long after the accomplices actually left.

I'm sure you've experienced going to an event for the first time and you consciously look at how other people are behaving and what they are doing becomes your guide for the way you should behave.

The following example of this in action I'm sure you can all relate to. Have you ever seen a new recruit join your organisation. They are bright eyed and bushy tailed. They are going to change the world!! Then in a couple of months they look like everyone else!! This wasn't a conscious decision they made, but they were influenced to be like the group norm they were part of. The culture influenced them to be like it.

All of these influences; culture, group and individual could influence us for good, for bad or it could be neutral. The point is that they do influence us and it is important to understand how and why so we can control the impact.

Activity

What are the influences on the people who will implement the commercial initiatives? How positive or negative are they and do they create the sort of culture that will result in commercial success?

EMOTIONS, ACTIONS, BEHAVIOUR

Imagine that something happens to you, let's keep it simple for the moment and say that, 'the something', is a senior colleague ignores you and doesn't talk to you. This event will affect your emotions and make you feel a certain way. This in turn will impact on your behaviour and actions.

However the process isn't actually as simple as this. There is a stage missing. An event occurring doesn't just impact on our emotions. It impacts on our emotions based on our interpretation of the event. Our mind is critical to the way we react to situations.

Let me give you an example: imagine you are at a conference and you really want to talk to the main speaker. You have read all of their books and love everything they say. It's a lunch break and you see the main speaker near you speaking to someone else. You decide to pluck up the courage to go and speak to them so you 'hover' near them waiting for them to finish their conversation. You know what it's like, you feel uncomfortable and awkward so you try and look natural and busy, perhaps busily checking your phone for that important message or looking across the room pretending you are trying to see someone else and you aren't really waiting next to the speaker ready to pounce!

You are standing just to the right of the speaker and they finish their conversation. They seem to look right past you, don't notice you, look to their left, see someone else and start talking to them.

This is 'the event', you were waiting to talk to the speaker, they don't notice you and they talk to someone else.

You could interpret this event a number of ways and it is this interpretation that will result in different emotions. You could interpret it as follows:

"I don't believe it. They don't want to speak with me. They saw me but just didn't want to speak with me. I don't blame them really, not many people want to speak with me. In fact no-one does really. There isn't much about me that would make people want to speak with me. I'm completely uninteresting, struggle for conversation and I always seem to bore people."

This interpretation of the event would lead to emotions of depression, lack of self-worth and possibly worse!

These emotions would in turn lead to a specific set of behaviours; most likely withdrawal, sitting by yourself and losing any motivation to speak with anyone.

Exactly the same event could be interpreted completely differently:

"Would you believe it? I was standing on their right and they looked to the left and saw someone they knew. What are the chances of that!"

This would lead to a whole new set of emotions; possibly increased determination and motivation to be more obvious so they don't 'slip through the net' next time. In turn the behaviours and actions could even involve doing star jumps right in front of the speaker so you definitely won't be overlooked next time. It could ultimately lead to a restraining order, but that's another issue!

So it isn't the event itself that impacts on our emotions and actions, but the combination of the event and the way we interpret it in our mind.

It is the same when looking at the way people and culture influence us. The people and the culture themselves aren't the only factors that lead to changes in our emotions and behaviour, but the combination of the people, culture and our interpretation. This means, to really understand how to get to grips with the way we are influenced personally and to ensure influences within our organisations are positive and conducive to commercial working, we need to look at both what is influencing us and our reaction and interpretation of it.

This perhaps means a different approach to leadership and management when we are working with people in commercial areas that are new to them. We have to find the time to coach them so they develop the confidence and the desire to see the initiatives work rather than let reactions overpower their behaviour and our view of them.

HOW IS CULTURE INFLUENCING US?

So the people we spend the most time with and the cultures we are in influence us, impact us and change us. This can be positive or negative but understanding it is important to produce engaged and productive teams that implement our commercial strategies.

It is normally easier to think about the way individual people influence us; looking at how culture impacts us can be much trickier as it is more subtle and can tap into such deeply held beliefs that we don't realise there is another way of thinking or acting.

Take the example of Joan of Arc. French culture had two deeply held assumptions at that time that completely influenced governmental decision making and life in general for the vast majority of French people. They were; that the English could never be beaten and that women could never do anything meaningful.

These paradigms of thinking were so deep that it wasn't talked about, it was just accepted and thoughts and actions came from a place of acceptance rather than questioning and challenging to see if it is true and if there is a different way to think.

It took a maverick, who was ultimately killed for being so radical, to challenge the paradigm and change the culture of France. It was because of Joan of Arc that the French finally realised the English could be beaten and eventually foreign and military policy changed and as a result the French gained freedom.

All organisations and groups have such paradigms. The unwritten and, often not thought about, assumptions that influence us and guide the way we act.

Often I find there are deeply held assumptions around the areas of commercial development such as:

- I will never be able to sell anything

- We will never be as successful as the private sector

- I'm not a commercial person

To really understand what forms and reinforces the culture of your organisations, and therefore what is influencing us, it is necessary to look a bit deeper. A useful model for doing this is the cultural web. This helps to identify what is creating and reinforcing the assumptions or paradigm that sits at the heart of the culture you are in. It does this by breaking it down into six different aspects.

The six aspects are:

Stories – not the formal communiques, but the informal stories that members of the group or organisation talk about in private.
- What core beliefs do stories reflect?
- How persuasive are these beliefs (through levels)?
- Do stories relate to:
    - Strengths or weaknesses?
    - Success or failure?
    - Conformity or mavericks?
- Who are the heroes and villains?
- What norms do the mavericks deviate from?

Routines and rituals of members of the group

- Which routines are emphasised?
- Which would look odd if changed?
- What behaviour do routines encourage?
- What are the key rituals?
- What core beliefs do they reflect?
- What do training programmes emphasise?
- How easy are rituals/routines to change?

Organisational structures of the group

- How mechanistic/organic are the structures?
- How flat/hierarchical are the structures?
- How formal/informal are the structures?
- Do structures encourage collaboration or competition?
- What types of power structure do they support?

Control systems of the group

- What is most closely monitored/controlled?
- Is emphasis on reward or punishment?
- Are controls related to history or current strategies?
- Are there many/few controls?

Power structures of the group

- What are the core beliefs of the leadership?
- How strongly held are these beliefs (idealists or pragmatists)?
- How is power distributed in the organisation?
- Where are the main blockages to change?

Symbols of the group

- What language and jargon are used?
- How internal or accessible are they?
- What aspects of strategy are highlighted in publicity?
- What status symbols are there?
- Are there particular symbols which denote the organisation?

This model applies to all organisations we are part of and the groups we associate ourselves with.

The culture that exists in our businesses impacts on the staff for good and for bad. It impacts on the way they make decisions, what they view as important and ultimately how they see themselves in relation to the vision of the organisation.

Activity

Have a go at creating your own cultural webs for your organisations and teams. Break the culture down to identify what is creating and reinforcing it. What are the influences that are not only forming the culture, but are also influencing you? What can you do about them?

Stories

Symbols

Power Structures

Organisational Structure

Control Systems

Routines and Rituals

The following true story shows how small changes in the stories that are told in an organisation, can change the culture and the underpinning paradigm.

The new CEO recognised there was a negative culture pervading the organisation and realised success depended upon doing something about it. The 'stories' that were told in the organisation were largely negative and that a 'glass half empty' philosophy dominated the business. He decided to change this by introducing a new approach that he started informally by modelling it himself before initiating it as company policy. He did this by simply starting every meeting with a good news story of something good that has happened in the company in the last week.

As good news became a more spoken about topic, he found that over about six months it eroded the power of the negative culture that existed. People began to think of 'what had gone well' ready for the next meeting they had to go to. The act of thinking differently, of allowing positive stories to influence them, made them change their outlook and actually be more positive.

The culture we are in influences us, so we have a responsibility to ensure the culture that is influencing us is as positive as possible. As leaders we have the responsibility to change the culture of our organisations so that it is positive for the people who are working for us. By doing so, the organisation will also achieve its purpose far more effectively and individuals will be engaged.

ENGAGING STAFF

A vast majority of the commercial opportunities that exist in the public sector rely on our people to make them succeed. Therefore working with our people; winning their hearts and minds is so important to the success of the initiative. The rest of this chapter includes sections of a previous book of mine: *Engaging Leadership Cultures*. This book looks at how we lead in a way to engage people; to win their hearts and minds and in so doing, increase productivity. Whilst this is important for leading in any organisation at any time, it is particularly important when developing new commercial initiatives which often involve asking people to work in new ways, to do new things, to carry on with the day job at the same time and in a climate of uncertainty. Their engagement is absolutely vital!

INVOLVEMENT AND EMPOWERMENT

For people to be truly engaged they have to be involved in things that impact on them. We see this time and time again on change programmes that we run. If people have been involved in the process and listened to, then they are far more likely to roll their sleeves up and join in with the implementation, even if they don't agree with the decision!

There was one particular change programme we ran for the Estates and Facilities department of a large NHS Trust, where this was very evident. The Director wanted to change things as he knew there were efficiency savings that could be made, but the department had been very resistant to change and used their experience and expertise in the areas of estates and facilities, to convince the Director, whose background wasn't in this area, that there was no way any change would work. Knowing this background we used the people from the department to design the change programme. Our role was to point them in the right direction and facilitate the process, but they did the work. In the end, the department, that had said no change was possible, found £2million savings from a £10million budget and delivered a better service at the end. They were involved and therefore they bought into it and made it far more successful that anyone envisaged.

To be engaged we also need to understand why we are important and significant. Why is our role vital to the bigger picture? If we understand why we are needed and significant, we are more likely to be engaged.

Involvement and empowerment have to be undertaken authentically for them to result in increased motivation and engagement. Many staff in large public sector organisations have a very cynical view of involvement. They are 'consulted' about changes, but in fact everyone already knows that the decision has been made. This form of 'consultation' is common and isn't about the organisation, it is normally about the leader. Their view of leadership is that as the leader, they are the one with the ideas and vision and therefore must ultimately make the decision, or have their way.

This type of involvement can be detrimental to the relationship that exists between the leader and everyone else. However the real impact of it is in the long term as it creates followers rather than new leaders. It tells people that their role is to serve the vision of someone else rather than have their own vision. It creates people who give the bare minimum and as a result are robbed of getting the most out of their time at work and who don't give their all.

We need to move from involvement and consultation to empowerment so we reproduce leaders who will have impact rather than followers who serve our visions.

A definition of empowerment that I quite like is that it is about; "sharing degrees of power with lower level employees to better serve the customer."

Empowerment is certainly about sharing power and not just sharing tasks. Very often we think we are empowering by delegating key tasks to people. However, the fact we are delegating tasks means we are not actually being empowering, we are just asking people to complete tasks that we have already thought about and planned. Instead we need to delegate authority. By delegating authority we are telling people; 'I trust you to do a good job here'. We are actually sharing power, a key aspect of this definition. The definition also has a second part; the power is shared for a reason and that reason is to serve an end goal; to better serve the customer.

The definition is saying, and rightly so, that the best way to serve a customer, which is the ultimate aim of the business, is to empower each staff member to make whatever decision is needed to serve the customer at that particular moment. Have you ever called a customer service department to solve a problem for you and there has been a really obvious solution that you have known and that the person on the other end of the phone has known as well? However, despite you both knowing this, the customer service rep hasn't been able to help you because they hadn't been given the authority to; it 'went against company processes'?

A few years ago I was driving to a client's offices and stopped to fill my car up with diesel. It was early in the morning and I mistakenly filled it up with petrol instead. I didn't realise to begin with and carried on driving for about half a mile until my car cut out on the side of the road. I called the break down service. They got to me really quickly and, whilst they were coming, I worked out what I had done. They towed me to the offices of the client I was working with that day, and arranged for their fuel truck to come and drain my fuel tank whilst I was working; brilliant service!

The fuel truck guy did what he had to do; I finished my days work and got back in the car to drive home. All was fine until halfway home my car stopped again. I waited three hours this time for the breakdown service. They got to me and found out that the fuel pump guy had put something back in my car the wrong way round. This meant I had been leaking diesel the whole way and I had broken down because I had run out of fuel.

The next breakdown guy was great as well. He gave me the number to call to put in a complaint and suggested that I should get a refund for the cost of the fuel I had lost and possibly the cost of the fuel pump work as it hadn't been done right and had led to a great inconvenience. In total this would have all come to about £300.

I duly followed the process he suggested, put in the complaint and was told to wait for an offer of compensation to be sent to me. I waited a week or so and finally a letter came in the post offering me £15 as a sign of goodwill! I wasn't too pleased and

I'm ashamed to say I didn't really feel the goodwill at that point in time! I called the company and ended up speaking to a customer service rep who had no authority to do anything other than to stick to the offer in the letter. It was one of the most frustrating phone calls I have ever had and it probably was for them as well. I clearly explained the inconvenience caused, the cost of the fuel I had lost and the fact it was because their staff hadn't done their job properly that all of this had happened. This last part wasn't quite true as if I had used the correct fuel in the first place the whole situation would have been avoided.

The poor customer service rep completely agreed with everything I said, but wasn't empowered to do anything beyond what the letter said. A few days later I spoke to their manager who had more authority and we reached a compromise somewhere between the two values. The manager had the authority to make that decision, which made me happy and meant that their job was actually far more pleasant than the original poor rep. I asked the manager why the original person wasn't able to do what they had done and I got the standard company reply; 'they don't have authorisation to do that sort of thing'.

If we delegate authority and empower people by giving away power, we actually achieve the end goals far more effectively. The end goals, based on the definition above, are providing the best service for customers. Given the definition of marketing we looked at earlier and the need to centre what we do around the customer rather than ourselves, empowering staff to provide service to customers is very important.

CREATING AN EMPOWERING ENVIRONMENT

Really empowering people as the norm is rare in my experience. People talk about it and do it in degrees, but really giving power and control away and taking the risk that goes with that is rare. Sometimes the leader at the top may do it, but people further down the organisational structure then become barriers to developing a truly engaging culture as they don't follow in the same path set by the leader. The following are important features of an engaging culture:

Transparent sharing of information – sharing information is important because it not only helps to build trust; it gives employees important information that will allow them to make the best possible decisions in critical situations. Communication, or sharing of information, is often the first hurdle to empowerment as 'information is power'. It is easy to slip into a subconscious mindset of controlling people through the power that is there because we have more information than they do. Often we use information to keep people down without realising it. We think it is the right thing to do. However, whatever the reason, it doesn't raise people up and empower them.

In many organisations I've worked with, senior managers keep much of the unpleasant information about a change programme to themselves, because they think their staff can't handle it. What they don't realise is that the biggest complaint of their staff is not that there will be some unpleasant changes, but that they are being treated like children as it is presumed that they can't cope with bad news.

A few years ago we had a piece of work for a large local authority. They had gone through a far reaching change programme and it was going very badly. At the root of the problem was gossip. Wherever you went in the organisation you heard gossip that; 'this is going to happen' or 'that is going to happen', 'they will change this next' or 'they will change that next'. No one knew exactly what was going to happen and in the absence of information, stories were made up that created fear, led to demotivation and resulted in productivity levels dropping massively. I'm sure that, if you've worked for a large organisation, you can relate to this story. In times of change the lack of information acts as a catalyst for gossip, fear and demotivation.

After university I took a year out and worked for a charity. My boss was a Glaswegian called Iain Bruce who had sayings about everything. One of them was; "when communication breaks down the imagination runs wild". This is so true and is exactly what happened in this case.

The local authority recruited a new interim Chief Executive who I will call Mike Jones for the purpose of this. He quickly realised that stopping the gossip was the single most important thing he had to do. He started to meet with all staff fortnightly, which was pretty much a full time job as there were around 12,000 staff. When he met with them he said; *"I'm going to be completely open and honest about everything that is going to happen and everything that is happening. If you ask me a question I will tell you the answer if I know it, even if you might not like the answer. However, in return I want you to do something for me. The next time you hear someone say something about the changes that are happening, say to them, 'did Mike Jones tell you that?' If they can't say yes or you don't believe them, then don't pass that information on."*

Quite soon you heard people regularly saying, "Did Mike Jones tell you that?" and it became a bit of a joke around the place. However it worked! Pretty soon Mike moved the meetings to monthly and then quarterly. Motivation increased and the whole programme got back on track. Why? Because information was used to empower people rather than control them.

Positive risk taking – we need to create a culture that says that it's OK to make mistakes, because it is only by making mistakes that we learn and we new things. Many of the organisations that I work with are crippled by fear. People won't try anything above and beyond the absolute standard because of fear that they will be blamed and possibly lose their job if it goes wrong. This has such a negative effect on people as the culture that develops stops them from being the people they could be.

Positive risk taking is about managing risk rather than completely avoiding it. The bigger mistake is often the over reaction from the original mistake.

Celebrate successes and failures – as part of creating a culture of empowerment we need to celebrate our successes and celebrate what we have learned from trying things that didn't work out. The act of trying something new should be encouraged and praised.

FOCUS ON STRENGTHS

A Gallup study found that when an organisation's leadership fail to focus on individuals' strengths, the odds of an employee being engaged are 1 in 11. But when an organisation's leadership focuses on the strengths of its employees, the odds of them being engaged increase to around 3 in 4. So when we focus on the strengths of those in our businesses they are far more likely to be engaged.

It sounds obvious; we are engaged by doing things we are good at. We only have to look at children to know this is true. Give them something they are interested in and they will do it for hours but if they aren't interested in it they will stick at for only a few minutes, unless they think they might get good at it.

My eldest daughter is a great, but pretty standard example of this. She loves swimming and wants to go swimming as often as possible. However, what she really loves about swimming is backstroke because she is particularly good and fast and wins her races. She is not nearly as good at butterfly and isn't nearly as engaged in these lessons as she is when the lesson is concentrating on getting even better at backstroke.

So it is pretty standard, common sense that we know intuitively; we are motivated and engaged by doing things we are good at. However most big organisations focus on exactly the opposite. They have a competency framework that people are assessed against based on their role and level in the organisation. Where the assessment shows they are weakest the focus of attention rests. It is in this area of weakness that people are trained, supported and coached so that they improve in the area of weakness. The result is standard people in standard roles who all complete the job safely and averagely.

Imagine what could happen if exactly the same assessment took place, but instead of finding the areas of weakness, the strengths were identified. Then development and training were given in the areas of strength so they became even better in those areas. Roles and responsibilities were moved around so that everyone spent more time doing things they were good at. Then each person would come alive and the productivity of the whole organisation would increase dramatically.

There was a great example of the value of understanding our strengths at the 2014 US PGA Golf championship. On the final round Rory McIlroy had lost his overnight one shot lead and was trailing by three shots after the first nine holes. On the par five 10th hole McIlroy drove the green in two shots, the only person in the whole tournament who managed to do so. He then putted for an eagle three catching up the leaders by two shots and creating the momentum that would see him go on and win the championship.

McIlroy's strength is driving straight and long. The rest of his golf game is also very good but it is this strength in driving that makes him unique, different and better than the opposition and it is this strength that is a focus of McIlroy in training. The rest of his game needs practice as weakness leads to failure, but it is our areas of strength that lead to success.

Our culture focuses on weakness due to an unhealthy fear of failure. However it is by focusing on strengths that people will come alive and we will succeed individually and corporately.

THE SCIENTISTS AND THE BIN MEN

A few years ago I was involved in two consulting projects running in parallel. The first was with the street cleaners and bin men of a city in England. The project was to introduce more efficient working processes and improve the effectiveness of the leadership team. The second was with a leading scientific organisation. They were the result of the merger of two previous organisations and the work was post-merger to develop a new single culture and efficient and productive working practices. The science undertaken quite literally blew me away and I certainly didn't understand it, but when someone shows you round the site and shows you kit that sounds like its from Star Trek you can't help but be impressed even if you have no idea what they are talking about!

On the surface the two projects looked very different; Bin Men in one project and some of the world's leading scientists in the other. However the issues with both projects largely came down to good people promoted into management without necessarily being good managers. In both cases we created improvement projects and identified an internal lead for each of the projects. We then did an exercise to identify and showcase the strengths of the teams. The project leads were then asked to choose people to help them on their projects based on what they now understood about each other's strengths.

I was leading on this part of the work for the project with the Bin Men and grown men quite literally cried as their peers recognised their strengths and chose them to help on the projects based on their unique strengths. Both projects were hugely successful and showed that focusing on strengths is incredibly powerful whatever your role, academic ability or walk in life.

New commercial projects often give us the chance to use people's strengths in a way that 'business as usual' doesn't.

Some of our strengths have been with us since we were born, others we discover, and in some cases they develop as we grow and mature. Ever since I was young, a strength of mine has been sport. It didn't matter what type of sport but as long as it involved running and a ball of some shape I have always had a natural talent for it and a passion to get even better. A particular strength I now have, which I didn't even know about until I started work as a consultant, is summarising. It sounds quite a small and niche strength, and it probably is, but I've found I have a natural ability. In one to one or group situations I am really good at taking in all of the disparate views and points and pulling it together into a concise summary of the discussion, conversation or agreement. This started off as a natural ability, as I had never been trained in it, and over time I have got better as I have pushed myself to do this in more challenging situations and with larger groups; all of which has helped me to turn this ability into a strength.

We need to understand our strengths so we can develop them further and we can use them more. There are some good tools available to help you identify your strengths but in the absence of them spend some time thinking through the following questions:

What natural talents / giftings / strengths do you have?

How do you currently use these strengths in your work?

What do you do to invest in these strengths and get even better in them?

What else could you do to invest in these strengths?

What could you do to use your strengths more?

LEADING OTHERS IN THEIR STRENGTHS

Marcus Buckingham suggests the world's greatest leaders believe that with enough development and investment, a person can achieve anything they set their mind to. Instead of helping people to overcome their weaknesses, great leaders find out what a person likes to do and is good at and empower them to do work they excel at.

We need to adopt the same approach. We need to help others to understand their strengths; we need to understand their strengths and we need to create opportunities for them to develop into these areas of strength.

Liz Wiseman found that great leaders are multipliers. They actually improve the intelligence and capabilities of those around them by two times. Multipliers look beyond their own ability and instead focus their energy on extracting and extending the ability of others. Wiseman found that they don't get a little more by doing this, they get vastly more. She found that leaders, whom she termed diminishers, stifled others and diluted the organisation's intelligence and capabilities. Effectively staff whose leaders were diminishers were working at 50% their capacity.

We become multipliers by focusing on the strengths of those around us and helping them to focus on their strengths as well. With a combination of concentrating on their strengths and helping them to understand their own vision, we will engage and enthuse our staff. To do this means we have to accept there will be mistakes and failure.

LOOK FOR STRENGTH NOT COMPETENCE

It is important not to confuse strengths with competence when looking for others' strengths so that you can invest in them. A strength comes from a natural ability or inclination and then needs further development to become a recognisable strength. This means that someone's area of strength may not be immediately recognisable because, in actual fact, they aren't that good at it yet in comparison to others.

So looking for strengths to invest in is not as simple as looking for things people are good at. If that were the case there would be no way anyone would develop into areas they had never tried!

IDENTIFY LIMITING EXPECTATIONS

The next part of the jigsaw is to ensure we have healthy expectations of what we are able to do. Having right expectations is so important to achieving our vision. Many studies prove this to be true; people who achieve are usually those who expect to achieve. So what do healthy expectations look like? How do we develop them and how can we lead others in a way so they also have healthy expectations of themselves?

There are a number of different facets to developing healthy expectations.

Bandura's theory of self-efficacy suggests that we limit ourselves by our own expectations. To put it simply; if we don't think we can achieve something then we are very unlikely to achieve it. I think it is perhaps easier to reflect on when the opposite is true, when we have a real deep down assurance we are going to succeed in something and that then comes to pass.

I particularly notice this phenomenon when playing golf, or rather trying badly to play golf. I stand at the ball with my club ready and I know before I swing the club whether it will be a good shot or whether I will fluff it. Why I know, I'm not sure. It could be because I am subconsciously working out whether I am standing correctly. It could be that actually the only thing that affects the shot is the thought in my head! If I think it will be a good shot, I relax and it generally is. If I think it will be a bad shot, I tense up and swing wrong. I don't know the reason, but I know it happens on multiple occasions when playing a round of golf. The more disconcerting thing is I still don't learn to stop the shot and start again when I do get these feelings!

A large amount of sports psychology is focused in this area; helping sports people believe that they have got what it takes to perform at the level required. In the work place the same phenomenon is also very evident. People who 'make it' in work, whatever that means, are seldom those who don't know how they did and never thought they would. People who rise to the top in work, sports and other areas of life are usually those who have a deep self confidence in who they are and the ability that they have.

An interesting study has been done looking at young ice hockey players in Canada. The study conclusively proved that children who had a birthday early in the school year are statistically far more likely to become a professional hockey player. The reason for this is as they are growing up they are the older kids in the year and therefore normally bigger than those whose birthday is later in the year. Size matters in hockey so in these early, formative years as a hockey player, they outperform those who are younger than them. Over time the physical difference disappears, but the self-confidence born from having out performed others remains. This results in a far higher proportion of those born early in the school year, becoming professional in comparison to those born later in the school year.

If our staff don't think they can 'work commercially' or if collectively there is an expectation that we won't meet the commercial objectives, then probably that will be proved right as the actions people take will be based on their expectations and will result in limiting behaviour and a self-fulfilling prophecy.

BALANCING EXPECTATIONS

In the work I have done in large organisations there seems to be a tipping point for leading other people's expectations. If we expect too much of them we overwhelm them and decrease their engagement. However, often we hold people back; we don't allow them to flourish or use their strengths and giftings and as a result, their self-expectations are greater than their ability to use their strengths and giftings. This also decreases engagement.

As leaders we have to find the tipping point. We need to push people who need pushing beyond their expectations, whilst supporting them. We also need to develop character in others whilst empowering them towards their expectations.

THE IMPACT OF LOSS

I've worked on, and been involved in, many change projects. They rarely seem to go smoothly as they are times of such heightened emotions. There was a particular project I was working on in which I came across a lady called Jeanette. She worked for an NHS Trust that was going through a fairly major change and reorganisation programme. She was a junior manager and had understood the need for the change and the logic and rationale behind the way it was being done. However she couldn't get her heart around it even though she understood it in her head.

After spending some time with her it emerged there were two main issues: the fact that what she was losing in the process, or that she perceived she was losing, was more important to her than the benefits of the programme. Secondly, the uncertainty that the change created was very unsettling for her. She was losing a support network of people she had grown to know and trust. As part of the change she was moving to a different part of the building to work with people she didn't know too well. It was probably a good opportunity for her, with greater career prospects and she knew that. However, it seemed the logical, rational benefits were outweighed by the sense of loss she was also experiencing.

To engage others we need to understand how and why people respond to change in the way they do and in fact we need to understand why we respond in the way that we do!

Kahneman and Tversky pioneered Prospect Theory which has since been the subject of many rigorous studies. Their findings have withstood the test of these studies and give us some interesting insights into the way humans work. The main principles behind prospect theory are:

Certainty: People have a strong preference for certainty and are willing to sacrifice potential gain to achieve more certainty. For example, if option A is a guaranteed win of £1,000, and option B is an 80 percent chance of winning £1,400 but a 20 percent chance of winning nothing, people tend to prefer option A.

Loss aversion: People tend to give losses more weight than gains — they're loss averse. So, if you gain £100 and lose £80, it may be considered a net *loss* in terms of satisfaction, even though you came out £20 ahead, because you'll tend to focus on how much you lost, not on how much you gained.

Understanding our desire for certainty, the fact we are loss averse and the impact fear has on us, gives us further clues about engaging with people's hearts and minds.

Consistency and certainty are strong driving forces in us humans. We want to know where we stand financially, in our relationships and in our work. Society is structured around having this kind of consistency and certainty. Most of us have a regular monthly salary that is needed to pay the regular monthly mortgage and other regular monthly bills. We budget based on our regular monthly income and outgoings. We hope for security in our jobs so that we can commit to these regular monthly commitments. We look to give certainty and consistency for our children by not moving around too much so they can stay in the same school etc.

None of this is wrong and in fact, more often than not, it is based on good wisdom and is an example of good stewardship of the things we have been given; money, resources and a family. However, it is also important to see it for what it is; a strong psychological desire to base our decision making on certainty rather than risk.

We make conservative decisions because the need for certainty is hard wired into our thinking. I am obviously generalising here and there are many people who buck this trend, however, for the majority of the population, this is how we think.

Whilst there is much wisdom and good stewardship that comes from this way of thinking, it also creates major problems when trying to change; individually and in workplaces. The reason it creates these problems is because our certainty is based largely on our experiences and therefore doesn't allow for new experiences with different results.

One of the most common factors that we come up against when trying to help implement a commercial development programme, is that people have already made up their mind about whether a programme is a good thing or not. This position is largely created from their experiences of previous programmes and their perception of what 'commercial' means. These experiences create expectations, both for the programme overall, and for the individual's own reaction to the changes. This sets the limit to their expected experience of the change. Put simply, if someone thinks the commercial change is rubbish, will be done badly and affect them emotionally, that is probably the way they will relate to the change because that is their expectation of it from the beginning.

In many businesses people have been so hurt by their previous experiences of change that the mere thought of it conjures up such powerful emotions that are far stronger than rational thought and decision making.

One of the most interesting parts of the example of certainty given is the perceived chance of winning nothing. In the example there was the chance of turning £1,000 into £1,400 but there was also a 20% chance of winning nothing. The percentage chance of winning nothing or losing is a judgement call we make and is coloured by our experiences. For example someone could think "my experience of the last change I went through was that it was done badly so I think the chance of winning nothing is 50% not 20%". Our perception of winning nothing, of being affected badly, is based on a judgement call that comes from our experiences and our personality.

The same is true when thinking about taking risks as we develop commercially. The percentage chance of 'winning nothing' is largely based on our previous experiences and self-expectations. For example I could think; "I won't call that company to try and make a sale because my experience tells me that my chance of 'not winning' and them not buying is high, so despite the fact it would be amazing if it did happen, I'm not going to do it. What's more I could look like a fool, what would people think of me?"

Does this pattern of thinking sound familiar? We perceive two areas of loss in this equation: firstly that the sale won't happen and secondly that others will think you are an idiot. This perception of loss reduces our perceived chance of winning and increases the attractiveness of maintaining the status quo and not stepping out and taking a risk.

The same goes for our attitude towards having difficult conversations with staff or managers or indeed anything else where we perceive there to be an element of risk.

The subconscious decision making process we go through tells us that the certainty we have in doing things the way we have always done them, is stronger than the potential increase we will get by taking a risk.

Other research undertaken suggests that the potential gain has to be twice that of the potential loss for people to consider the risk worth taking. In the experiment people were given a 50/50 chance of either winning or losing money. People would only take that chance if the amount they might win was worth twice the value of what they might lose.

LOSS AVERSION

The other part of Prospect Theory, loss aversion, is interesting as it provides another insight into human nature. An interesting experiment was done in London's Spitalfields Market by the BBC programme Horizon. Strangers were approached and given £20 and offered the chance to increase that to £50 by betting it against a roulette wheel.

This was the basic scenario, but it was put to people in two different ways. In the first scenario people were given £20 and told they could stick with the £20 or they could use it to bet and possibly turn it into £50. The vast majority of people approached using this method, stuck with the £20.

The second way people were approached was slightly different. They were given £50 and immediately had £30 taken away. They were told they could win it back by betting the £20 they still had. Looking at this rationally it is the same scenario. People ended up with £20 they didn't have before and were told they could either keep it or use it to gamble with to possibly gain another £30.

However, because of the different way the scenario was put to the people, the results were totally different. One group had the full £50 in their hands to begin with, so when £30 was taken away from them they felt they had lost something. The majority of people approached using this scenario decided to gamble the money compared to a very small percentage of people using the other scenario.

Most people are more concerned about keeping what they've got than gaining something they have never had. We worry more about loss than gain. As leaders we must be aware of this in ourselves so we don't pass opportunities for promotion over. We also must be aware of this in the way we lead our people.

FEAR

There are many potential sources of fear for a leader: a lack of self-confidence, imposter syndrome (feeling that you are a fake and blagging it), a culture in your work environment of coming down hard on failure, tough market conditions that make every decision vital, a worry for the future or worry of what others will think of you. A good staging post for dealing with fear is to focus on stopping the symptoms of fear affecting our leadership.

By focusing on stopping the symptoms of fear we will, over time, change our habitual way of thinking and reduce the impact of fear on our leadership.

THE SYMPTOMS OF FEARFUL LEADERSHIP

We disempower others as our power decreases - the leader takes more and more upon their own shoulders as they don't trust others to achieve the same results they could or because they feel threatened by gifted people in their workplaces. This decreases engagement by reducing involvement and autonomy. Empowering others to use and develop their gifts and strengths and involving others in key decisions are all motivating factors that increase engagement in workforces and, in so doing, move people towards living a full life.

Giving others autonomy is also proven to be a highly motivating factor, whilst disempowering staff reduces their involvement and autonomy. One of the personal characteristics of engaging leaders is that they are trustworthy and they trust others. The likelihood is that trust is also undermined by disempowering others.

The strength of relationships decrease – when the leader draws everything closer to themselves and are less trusting and authentic in their relationships, it decreases engagement by reducing trust in the relationships and changing the values of the relationship. Trust is again the main characteristic that will be eroded by succumbing to fear in leadership. Followers will feel they aren't trusted and in turn the trust they have in their leader will decrease. A change in the strength of relationships says quite a bit about the values, particularly the informal values that are evident in the workplace. When we see alignment between our personal values and the formal and informal values of the workplace we are more engaged and more a part of it. The converse is also true!

The quality of decisions decreases as our self-control decreases - the leader's emotional intelligence is reduced and they have less awareness of the impact they have on others, less empathy with others and less self-control. This decreases engagement by reducing trust and hope. We also become less stable in the way we respond to people as our self-control is reduced, which again decreases their engagement and connection. When emotional intelligence is reduced, our ability to control our self is also reduced, leading to instability. Hope and compassion; two other important characteristics of engaging leaders also decrease as fear affects decision making.

THE IMPACT OF FEARFUL LEADERSHIP

An obvious impact on people when fear becomes a part of our decision making is a reduction in engagement and connection. This becomes a vicious cycle; as fear increases, connection drops further which reinforces this unhealthy loop. The less obvious impact is that we never become the leader we could be.

We don't reach our potential and have the impact we could have because we are hamstrung by letting fear affect our thinking.

The opposite of fear based leadership is empowering leadership, based on good relationships and emotional intelligence. To have power and be powerful is to give it away and empower others. To demonstrate compassion in the workplace is to build good relationships. Self-control or high levels of emotional intelligence have been shown by Daniel Goleman to be the main distinguishing factor that separates great leaders with average leaders. Staff not being empowered by defensive leaders, relationships breaking down and leaders who lack self-control and awareness of the impact they have on others, are three of the most common problems I see across businesses of all types and are some of the main reasons there are unfulfilled people in our workforces. The root of this is fear.

To be engaged and to engage others we must recognise there are some patterns of thought that are natural to us, which are actually counter-productive to developing engaged and productive workforces that grasp the challenge of developing commercially.

PERSONAL CHARACTERISTICS OF LEADERS

It is easy to see how our personal characteristics effect the engagement of others with the commercial development agenda. The culture we create through our example and the decisions we make has direct consequences in others' lives and therefore impacts on their engagement.

The research we have done has found the leadership culture that exists in organisations to be the single biggest factor that impacts on this engagement. This means it is also the biggest factor influencing the productivity of the organisation and the likelihood to successfully implement new commercial strategies. This culture is set by us, the leaders.

Some really interesting research has been undertaken by Gallup looking at the personal characteristics of leaders that have the most engaged followers. Their premise is that to find out what leadership characteristics engage people, the ones to ask are not the leaders, but the followers of leaders. What is it about their leaders that engages or disengages them?

They conducted this research globally between 2005 and 2008, initially with around 10,000 people, creating a strong and robust research base to draw conclusions from. They asked people to think of a leader who has the most positive effect on their daily life and then to think of what this person contributes to their life.

They concluded there are four characteristics that are more important than any others in engaging followers. Engaged followers means two things, firstly that they are enjoying their work; secondly, that they are more productive so the organisation, of whatever type, achieves more.

The four characteristics they found to be so important are; trust, hope, compassion and stability.

TRUST

Gallup found the chance of an employee being engaged at work if they don't trust the company's leaders is 1 in 12. However the chances of an employee being engaged if they do trust the company's leaders are better than 1 in 2. This is more than a six fold increase and will have a corresponding impact on productivity, performance and the life that the employee is living.

So what is it that leads to trust or in fact distrust. At a very obvious level if the leader is a liar or found to be unethical in the decisions they make, then trust is eroded. However the picture is actually far more complex than that. I'm sure many of you have worked with leaders who have the best intentions and want to give the best results for their staff. The result of this is they can often over promise. They say they will do things and have the best intentions to do them, but never quite deliver against what they say they will do. This might come from a good place, but actually the effect is the same; trust is eroded.

Stephen M.R. Covey, in his book; The Speed of Trust identifies four key components of Trust: integrity, intent, capability and results. The first two are internal factors that others judge us by whilst the second two relate to our performance and whether others will trust us to do a certain task based on their perception of our ability and track record.

Every year Edelman conducts a global study of trust looking at levels of trust in 26 countries in government, business, NGOs and the media. Part of their research involves looking at how much people trust the leaders in these four different spheres of society. To measure this they have created the Edelman Trust Barometer. The Trust Barometer identifies 16 specific attributes which build trust and clusters them into five groups; engagement, integrity, products and services, purpose and operations.

When going through the checklist, a useful question to ask might be; 'how would others score me in these areas'? Try and put yourself in their shoes. If you're really brave, perhaps ask them to score you, but make sure you give them permission to be completely honest and don't get defensive at the results if they are not what you expected!

Score yourself between 1 and 5 for these 16 attributes with 5 being very good and 1 very poor.

Listens to customer needs and feedback

Treats employees well

Places customers ahead of profits

Communicates frequently and honestly on the state of the business

Has ethical business practices

Takes responsible actions to address an issue or crisis

Has transparent and open business practices

Offers high quality products and services

Is an innovator of new products, services or ideas

Works to protect and improve the environment

Addresses societies' needs in everyday business issues

Creates programmes that positively impact on the local community

Partners with NGOs, government and 3rd parties to address societal needs

Has highly regarded and widely admired top leadership

Ranks on a global list of top companies

Delivers consistent financial returns to investors

TOTAL

TRUST AND CULTURE

It is interesting and useful to look a bit deeper into the Edelman report as it shows some cultural trends in trust that identify some of the barriers we might face as we look to build trust.

Levels of trust vary from country to country, ranging from a score of 80 for China, down to 36 for Russia. The scores reveal, not only the way business is done or perceived to be done in these countries, but also the levels of trust in the different cultures. The culture of trust that exists in a country will have an impact on the levels of trust in your organisation. Individuals are impacted on by the prevailing culture and as a result, view events, organisation and people through the lens of that culture. Both the US and UK come in the middle of the league table of trust. The US scored 59 and the UK 53 in the last survey.

HOPE

Gallup's research found that 69% of employees who feel enthusiastic about the future are engaged in their jobs compared to 1% who are not enthusiastic about the future. Instilling hope in people is a foundational requirement for leading. Hope allows people to see beyond their current circumstances towards something better. Having a vision for the commercial initiative rather than just trying to be cost neutral to avoid job losses, is one important aspect of creating hope for the future.

We need to spend time deliberately creating hope for the future and positioning ourselves to also be hopeful. This can be a challenge and in my experience there are two main barriers to doing this:

- Busyness, reacting to the needs of today

- Difficult and uncertain futures

It is difficult to give hope in situations that seem hopeless. Many of our clients have gone through large restructures and cost cutting exercises recently and, as a result, made many people redundant. It is very hard for a manager to give hope in these circumstances and even harder to do it in a genuine and authentic way that doesn't undermine the trust staff have in them. Trust that is very important as we have just read!

Creating and communicating hope for others requires us to be proactive. Hope comes from looking to the future not by responding to the needs of today. Many of us are pretty bad at this and are getting worse. 'Busyness syndrome', as it is being coined, is affecting all walks of life and actually reducing our productivity let alone our ability to convey hope to others.

Busyness syndrome seems to be created from three sources:

1. Finding self-worth through being busy and letting others know how busy we are

2. Poor skills of prioritisation, focusing our time on low priority tasks that are perhaps urgent but not important rather than important tasks that perhaps don't have the same deadlines

3. A culture of now and of distractions - we expect replies quickly, we get messages immediately on our phones and tablets all of which makes it easier to respond to small, less urgent tasks.

Try and identify areas of hopelessness in your business. What is the assumption behind the hopelessness? The following are examples of lies I hear all of the time in businesses:

- The market is too hard, the clients just don't spend money any more

- The competition can do this better than we will ever be able to

- This change will go badly because they always do and no one likes change

You get the idea. Identify the hopelessness, then identify the assumption that sits behind the hopelessness and challenge the assumption. Is there are different way of looking at the situation?

COMPASSION

The most productive companies have a leadership culture that focuses on developing and recognising staff, encouraging open feedback and promoting teamwork.

According to research by Christina Boedker, from the Australian School of Business, out of all of the various measurements they looked at in an organisation, the ability of the leader to be compassionate – that is, *"to understand people's motivators, hopes and difficulties and to create the right support mechanism to allow people to be as good as they can be"* – that had the greatest correlation with profitability and productivity.

The field of research that I am involved in, behavioural economics, is demonstrating quite clearly that the old "command and control" style of leadership is not nearly as effective as a "connect and collaborate" style.

Those that lead by intimidation might appear to get results, but the results end up being short-term, and often cause anxiety in others. This leads to poor workplace morale and staff who either leave the company prematurely, fail to work at their best or become saboteurs. The same is true if you tone down the word 'intimidation' to, leading by the force of their personality. They could be very nice people who are great fun to work with, but a focus on task as opposed to relationship will not get the same results in the long run.

In the past, a compassionate style of leadership was seen as weak. However demonstrating compassion, whilst still meeting hard targets and objectives, is actually far more challenging than a more autocratic style of leadership.

BUT WHAT DOES COMPASSION MEAN?

When we talk about compassion in the workplace, it is easy to mistake it for letting people get away with things and not having the difficult conversations that need to be had. This isn't compassion at all. Compassion is about making those difficult decisions and tackling poor performance, but with a focus on wanting the best for the person and helping them to become the best that they can be. This sometimes means compassionately letting people go.

Avoiding difficult conversations and letting people get away with things, is actually the opposite of being compassionate as it isn't helping them be their best and is probably also being unfair on others who have to work harder to make up for the performance of those that aren't pulling their weight.

I designed a change programme a few years ago for a large disabled rights charity. They had a policy that they would actively provide employment opportunities for disabled staff, as it was in line with the values of the organisation. However, there was a perception that the disabled staff were allowed to get away with more than the able bodied staff which led to a divide, reduced engagement and ultimately bad relationships and poor performance. The 'compassion' shown to those disabled staff actually back fired as it resulted in a perceived lack of compassion for the able bodied staff.

The following are seven characteristics of compassionate leadership. As you read them try and identify areas that you can work on to become more compassionate.

Listen, listen and listen again- compassionate leaders listen more than they talk. When making tough decisions and facing bad news they don't jump to conclusions but gather more information.

Assume the best in others – a quote I heard recently although I'm not sure where from, is that when thinking of others we judge their behaviour, when thinking of ourselves we judge our motives. We need to judge others as we judge ourselves and see why they are doing what they are doing and what they are trying to achieve.

Keep your emotions in check – We need self-control so that we relate to others as we would plan, not as we would react.

Be interested in others – show that you are genuinely interested in others not just asking questions without really listening. People see through a lack of authenticity so you really do have to be interested in others for them to think you are interested in them!

Accept responsibility – According to Brian Tracy, the motivational guru, the hallmark of a fully mature human being is to be 100% responsible for our lives. Blaming others and creating excuses for our mistakes is one of the primary causes for failure as adults and a contributor to poor mental health. It is only when we accept responsibility that we are able to repent and forgive.

Be open to feedback – feedback shows us the impact of our actions and opens our eyes to things we are not aware off. We must learn to rejoice in feedback, weigh it, accept the useful parts, change things based on useful feedback and not allow feedback to damage us.

Support others in their vision – we must focus on helping each person be the best they can be, whether that is in their career or something else!

STABILITY

People want to follow someone who provides a solid

foundation; it gives them stability to be with other people who provide stability. The stability that people are looking for is largely emotional stability. To provide this we need to know how people will react to situations. I used to work for someone who, when things were going well, was great fun and a joy to work with. When he was stressed, you knew it was time to head for cover as you could see the vein start throbbing on the side of his head and you knew his self-control was reduced. This led to many unhealthy conflict situations and some questionable decision making. The effect across the company was reduced motivation and a work force who didn't really want to be there.

Stability means we are emotionally self-aware, in control of emotional expression, secure, and positive. Many studies have found that emotional intelligence, which includes the characteristics just mentioned, is the biggest determinant as to whether a leader will be successful or not.

What kind of stability do you give those around you? Read the following five statements. Then use a 1-5 (low-high) scale to rate your level of agreement:

___ I have good self-control; I don't get negatively emotional and angry.

___ I perform well under pressure.

___ I'm an optimistic person who sees the positive side of situations.

___ I give people lots of praise and encouragement; I don't put people down and criticise.

___ I view myself as being relaxed and secure, rather than nervous and insecure.

It is our staff that make the commercial initiatives work. Therefore leading in a way that wins their hearts and minds is so important. Our personal characteristics impact on our staff. In fact they are a large determinant in the engagement of those in our businesses. We need to be trustworthy and trusting. We need to give hope. We need to be compassionate and we need to be stable and emotionally mature.

By developing these characteristics our staff will be more engaged and in fact we also become more engaged as well.

14.

MARKETING

Most of what has been covered in this book so far is becoming part of the role of a modern manager in the public sector. However, I also think there are some specialisms that are new functions public sector organisations will have to develop in order to succeed commercially. These include market analysis, marketing and sales. In this chapter we will explore marketing to a degree. This will in no way be a comprehensive guide to marketing, as there are many books on that subject, but instead it will look at some of the most important elements for successfully marketing services based on some of the most common mistakes I have seen whilst working in this environment. Later on in this chapter I include an example of a tactical marketing plan that can be used as a template for structuring your marketing plans.

THE ONE-OFF MARKETING CAMPAIGN

Fairly frequently I come across despondency and helplessness. The commercial unit has undertaken a marketing campaign and it hasn't worked and they don't know what else to try. Sometimes this marketing campaign will have cost them quite a bit, particularly if it included advertising, and always it will have taken time and effort. Very often the campaign has been based on the solid foundations of a segmented marketing strategy and a targeted approach based on a particular segment. It's been done right and yet still doesn't work!

The reason for this is because of a lack of understanding about the process people go through to make a buying decision and an unrealistic expectation that if you've segmented right and targeted the segments with the right offer – how could they refuse!

The reality is that people might not be ready to buy when they first hear from you. Even if they are ready to buy, they may currently get the service from someone else and they might not be ready to change supplier to you. Very rarely in marketing is there a silver bullet that produces amazing results immediately. Marketing is a process that, when done well, increases results over time. There are three words that are useful to remember when thinking about developing a marketing campaign. They are:

- Recency

- Frequency

- Potency

Recency – a prospective customer is more likely to buy from you if they have recently heard from you when they are ready to buy. The one off campaign takes a large risk that; either the customer is ready to buy or that they will remember us when they are. As other competitors are probably also contacting them and they have many other priorities that are nothing to do with the product we are offering, the reality is that they will probably forget about our one-off campaign very quickly. The more recently they have heard from us, the more likely they are to remember us and therefore the more likely they are to enquire from us about our products and services. The implication is that for our customers and potential customers to have heard from us recently, we have to communicate with them often!

Frequency – a prospective customer is more likely to buy from you if they frequently hear from you. The more they hear from you the more they become familiar with your brand, your product, your offer etc. Familiarity builds up trust and over time, that familiarity may be enough to make them take a risk and get a quote from you. The more frequently they hear from you the more likely they are to remember you when they are in a position to buy. The implication of this is that you must contact them repeatedly rather than through a one off campaign if you expect to see results.

Potency - a prospective customer is more likely to buy from you if your message is in line with their need. This is where customer segmentation and A/B testing come in. If you've segmented your market well then you know the needs and desires of the different segments. Each segment requires a different campaign and each segment requires that campaign to be repeated many times in order to see success. A/B testing is where you test different messages within the segment to see which gets a better response. Do more of what works and less of what doesn't!

The implication of these three words, as you've probably already sussed, is that effective marketing requires a continuous segmented campaign where customers are contacted each and every month. Over time the number of leads resulting from each campaign will increase as your message becomes more prominent in the minds of customers and hits them when they are ready to make a purchasing decision. This applies to all forms of marketing and advertising. In fact it is particularly important to consider this when advertising as bad advertising is probably the best way of wasting your budget! It costs a lot and a one off advert online, in a newspaper or on the radio is very unlikely to deliver results as customers may take no notice and might not be in a position to buy at that point in time. When they are ready they will have forgotten about you!

THE USP

The other common mistake I see is an unhealthy focus on trying to have a unique selling point (USP). There seems to be a common misconception that we must be unique in order to win customers. Taken to the extreme this leads to marketing messages focused around perceived unique features that in fact the customer couldn't care less about! It is much better to have nothing unique and focus on doing well that which is important to customers than it is positioning yourself around a USP that is peripheral at best from the customer's perspective.

WEBSITES AND SOCIAL MEDIA

Social media marketing can often be the most cost effective form of marketing, however it must be done well and in a responsive way. I've seen many examples of social media campaigns that generate comments, both positive and negative, but there is no interaction with these comments from the service itself. People expect interaction and without it the campaign could well be counterproductive.

Make sure the customer can find your website easily, navigate through it without any difficulty and follow a call to action online. So many commercial services are located on the main corporate website. Whilst this itself is not necessarily a problem, if finding it and navigating to it is difficult for the customer then they just won't bother! Once on the website, make sure as much as possible is automated. If they can't join, pay or buy online then they very well might not bother to make that phone call or print off and complete the membership form. I know because I wouldn't! In today's age customers expect to be able to complete the whole interaction online. If they can't they won't make much of an effort.

Make sure your website is prepared for this before undertaking any marketing campaign or else the hard work of a marketing campaign could well be wasted through your poor website capability.

THE TACTICAL MARKETING PLAN

In order to pull all this together, a tactical marketing plan is required that lays out how the marketing will be undertaken. The SOSTAC planning model I find very useful for doing this. SOSTAC is an acronym that stands for:

- Situation (where we are now)

- Objectives (where we want to get to)

- Strategy (how do we get there

- Tactics

- Action

- Control

Much of the information you will have generated developing your business case through the tools and techniques laid out earlier in this book will help feed into this plan.

Following is an annotated example of a SOSTAC Tactical Marketing Plan taken from a local authority Pest Control service. The example will show how to turn this thinking into something practical that will help you win customers and deliver against your objectives.

PEST CONTROL MARKETING PLAN

The following tactical marketing plan uses the SOSTAC model to suggest an approach that is designed to deliver against the identified objectives over a five year period. Success will come by sticking to the broad strategy whilst developing the nuances of the campaign over time.

SITUATION

XXXX District Council currently has a PEST Control service that generates income. Over the coming years the service must generate higher levels of income and has the opportunity to create a small, but successful Pest Management business.

The Pest control market in the UK is growing and there is local opportunity as the market analysis below describes:

UK market trends

There is a growing market for pest control in the UK with total revenue of £389m last year across 609 businesses, with an annual growth rate of 4.4% between 2010 and 2015 (data from Ibis World market research). Ibis World summarize that:

"The Pest Control industry has been doing well. Although the structure of the industry has been changing due to the decline of services provided through councils, private firms have still managed to attract sufficient business to expand."

Headline statistics

- *Revenue: £389m*

- *Annual growth (2010-2015): 4.4%*

- *Businesses: 609*

- *Employment: 6,459*

When extrapolated down and applied to XXXX, this would mean an estimated local market with local revenue of £737,944 per year.

There have also been clear themes in the UK market with a significant increase in competition, led mainly from the reduction of council services operating at a free or significantly subsidised rate. On top of that there has been an increasing use of environmentally friendly and humane methods of pest control, matching a rise in environmentally conscious consumers throughout the UK. The rise in small operators, usually one or two people, is particularly noticeable in the pest control sector.

Headline themes

- *Large increase in market competition*

- *Increase in humane and environmentally friendly methods.*

Local market

There is a segmented market for local pest control that divides into three main groups:

- *Large, well known, nationwide firms such as Rentokil who are more expensive at both domestic and commercial levels.*

- *Small operators, usually one or two people operating locally at varying prices below the large firms and of varying degrees of effectiveness.*

- *Specialist companies, again usually of smaller scale that concentrate on more complicated and specialised procedures, such as for bees.*

The large firms have largely locked down the chain stores such as supermarkets and high street retailers, who operate under centrally controlled contracts at scale. Whilst there was some desire from managers to negotiate because not all were happy with the level of service provided, most said it was out of their hands when we spoke to them via phone conversations.

The small firms are predominantly "man with a van" type operations and vary in the quality and range of services provided. Most get by on word-of-mouth, some smaller contracts with local businesses and on Google searches or phone directory look-ups. Again, when calling local businesses their satisfaction with current services varied significantly from perfectly happy with current levels to very disappointed. These businesses' willingness to discuss their contracts, however, was almost exclusive and if a better price was available then many would be willing to switch. A lack of any sort of sizeable sales and administrative team for most of these types of businesses also hampered their ability to respond quickly to call outs and queries. Likewise, their capacity to get to people quickly was restricted to their workload. Often waits of up to 72 hours for pest control services were reported when test calls were made.

There were a small number of specialist companies offering services based heavily around a type of pest control, usually moles or bees. They work almost exclusively on one type of pest control, aiming to build up a loyal following, with repeat business. It was not clear how this group were affected by fluctuations in, for example, wasp infestations.

Quite a few of the neighbouring Local Authorities don't offer a commercial Pest Control service or indeed have disbanded their service altogether.

OBJECTIVES

The vision is to create a regional business over the next five years that turns over £500,000/annum with 20% profit levels. The business will operate across the XXXXX region spreading geographically from its XXXXX base.

STRATEGY

In order to achieve the objectives laid out in the market conditions described above the strategy should be very focused and intentional. There are three strands to this strategy:

1. *Market penetration of the local commercial market*

2. *Market penetration of the local domestic market*
3. *Market extension into neighbouring geographical markets*

Ansoff Matrix

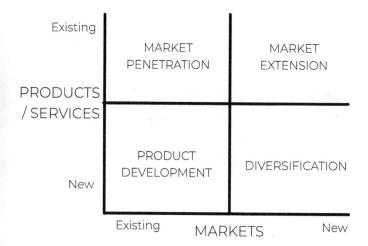

The focus for all three parts of this strategy is on the core product of Pest Control rather than to develop new products or services that are outside of the core of the business. The market analysis shows that there is a large local market so effort should be made to make further inroads into that with any spare capacity the service has.

A strategy of market penetration focuses existing products and services on existing markets to increase the market share in that market. A strategy of market extension looks to take existing products and services to new markets.

1. Market penetration of the local commercial market

This part of the strategy will look to increase the number of pest control contracts with small to medium sized businesses within the XXXXX Council geographical boundary. The small to medium sized business are seen as the target market as the large ones are part of larger groups with their pest control services tied up as part of a larger national contract.

2. Market penetration of the local domestic market

The focus of operations to date has been to increase the commercial side of the business due to the high rates paid and the nature of the business – planned preventative in the commercial market and emergency call out in domestic.

The future strategy should include the domestic market for two reasons:

- *There is a large market and greater penetration in the market will increase achievement towards targets*

- *Increasing penetration in this market will increase brand awareness increasing the chances of gaining planned preventative commercial contracts*

The market analysis shows that XXXXX Council currently charges a long way below the market rate, in fact at a rate less than it costs them to deliver the service.

The price should be brought up to the market rate for two reasons:

- *Charging a low price will damage the brand and hinder the ability to gain commercial contracts*

- *A quality service is provided and there should be fair compensation for that service*

3. Market extension into neighbouring geographical markets

Many of the neighbouring local authorities don't provide a pest control service. The XXXXXX Council pest control service should extend into these geographical markets. This should be a staged approach:

- *Focus on those areas that neighbour XXXXXX to begin with so operations can still all be controlled in the existing way.*

- *Focus on planned preventative commercial contracts which are more profitable and will enable 'rounds' to be planned to minimise travelling time.*

- *In the future new business models should be explored that will enable greater levels of work in geographical areas further away from XXXXX.*

TACTICS

A general ethos that sits behind the tactics for all three strategic areas is the same. That is there is no 'magic' formula or message that will create market demand and increase business, but a planned and continual campaign will result in meeting the business objectives.

For all three areas it is suggested that a combination of direct marketing and follow on sales will give the best long term results. The 'actions' section of this report suggests a campaign timetable that should be manageable and will deliver the results needed.

The thinking behind this approach is that people don't buy when they first hear a message. They buy when they need the service and when they remember the message. This leads to three golden rules of direct marketing:

- *Recency – people buy when they've heard the message recently*

- *Frequency – people buy when they have frequently heard the message*

- *Potency – people buy when the message matches their need and values*

The tactics behind growing strategy 1 and 2 is very similar and follows two strands:

- *A segmented continuous direct marketing campaign*

- *A concerted focus on identifying and winning large contracts*

- *Cross selling through referrals*

A segmented continuous direct marketing campaign

A continuous direct marketing campaign should be developed for both the local market and the geographical areas the business is looking to move into. This should use the following steps as a guide:

1. *Develop or buy database of businesses in the local area*

2. *Segment the database into key customer segments which have similar characteristics (food retailers, schools, part of a larger national company etc.)*

3. *Develop marketing material that focuses on the key needs of the target segments*

4. *Send marketing materials to them on a monthly basis*

5. *Use marketing material to gain sign-ups for a newsletter*

6. *Send monthly newsletter – tracking interest in particular features*

7. *Follow up leads*

There are a few key points that underpin this process:

XXXXX already has many business contacts and through Food Standards and links to Schools it is possible to develop a database very quickly.

The database should continually be updated and improved.

Key decision makers names should be sought rather than generic enquiry addresses – this may require work on the telephone to develop the best database in the first instance.

The marketing materials could be sent via post or email. Both should be tried and the results recorded.

The message of the marketing material is vitally important. It must focus on what is important to the customer groups. The success of different messages should be recorded so the impact of the messages is understood.

The newsletter should be genuinely news worthy offering advice and tips to make people want to read it. Using a platform like MailChimp it is possible to get them looking good and to track opens and clicks to determine interest and qualify leads.

A concerted focus on identifying and winning large contracts

Winning large contracts enables resources to be increased and linked to known income levels and is therefore very attractive. To win the larger contract a relationship management approach should be taken as people buy from other people. The process adopted should be as follows:

1. *Develop a list of the businesses that you would like to work with*

2. *Identify the key decision makers in the business through desk based research and telephone work*

3. *Contact them to arrange a meeting or to send marketing collateral through to*

4. *Follow up on a monthly to bi-monthly basis*

A key point to note is the need for realism when it comes to identifying the business you would like to work with. Currently the Pest Control services only delivers relatively small sized contracts. Most businesses are likely to ask for example of delivering similar types of work to the work they are looking to commission. Therefore the initial list should be for contracts likely to be bigger than they ones currently undertaken, but of a similar scale. As these are won then the next size up can be chased. This will ensure an efficient approach to this element of the work rather than spending time chasing work that is very unlikely to be won in the near future.

Cross selling through referrals

A competitive advantage held by the Pest Control Service is the link to other council services that also provide support to businesses. This is something that should be utilised.

Trade Waste customers should be offered an introductory deal for Pest Management. This shows added value by being a Trade Waste Customer, but also utilises the links across similar council services.

The processes adopted should be simple for the customer. Therefore direct debits and card payments should be possible and a website dedicated to the business services should also be developed to make it easy for customers to find the information they are looking for. The main council website should maintain information about the service, but should link to a new dedicated website.

ACTION

It is envisaged that work will start in earnest once the new commercial team is in place. The three roles in the new commercial team will operate as follows:

Commercial analyst – will work on developing the data based and identifying the potential larger contracts. They will also have a role in send out the monthly sales communication and developing the newsletter.

Business Development Officer – will play a role in the monthly sales letter, the newsletter and in following up leads with a face to face visit.

Commercial Development Manager – will oversee the process and be the key relationship manager for potential larger projects

The most important aspect of this campaign is that it happens on an ongoing basis. This requires disciplined management and action.

At this point there would be a detailed action plan specifying who is doing what and when.

CONTROL

Outputs and outcomes must both be controlled in order to refine the campaign as it goes along.

Output measures

- *The frequency that potential customer are contacted should be measured and controlled.*

- *The number of potential customers contacted each campaign should be measured.*

Outcome measures

- *The number of leads generated in each customer segment and with each message used should be measured. This information should feed into future campaigns to do more of what is working.*

- *The conversion rate of leads should be measured.*

- *The effectiveness of moving leads through a sales pipeline should be measured.*

- *The income generated.*

- *The profit generated.*

The tactics of marketing is an enormous subject in its own right and isn't the focus of this book, but hopefully this example gives you a template to develop the tactical plan you need to go alongside a commercial strategy. The tactical plan turns ideas into reality.

COMMERCIAL GOV

15.

STRUCTURE AND GOVERNANCE

Many of the questions I get asked focus on the right structure or mechanism for developing a commercial entity. There seems to be a feeling that if we get the right entity then success will follow. I agree with this to a degree. Setting things up right in the first instance has a big impact on the subsequent success. However, choosing the entity should come after a thorough strategic analysis of the options, the market and the objectives. Structure should always serve the strategy which in turn should serve the mission.

Often the reason behind the question is a frustration at the barriers people have come across whilst trying to get their commercial initiatives off the ground and operating as they could and should do. In essence the internal bureaucracy has led people to think that an arm's length wholly owned company is the Holy Grail. It might be the right solution, but it is one of many options. Many people who work in this field, myself included, think that one of the main benefits of an arms length company is purely to free commercial initiatives from internal bureaucracy, but if there is another way to achieve that then it could be just as effective, and sometimes quicker, with less work entailed. Following on in this chapter I will outline some of the legislative background that enables the public sector to trade and some of the structural options for doing that. I'm not a lawyer and this is in no way legal advice on what is right for you. It will hopefully highlight some of the issues and options that you have.

The following information is adapted from a guide around trading produced by the Local Government Association (LGA).

The Localism Act 2011 introduced the General Power of Competence (GPC), which explicitly gave councils the power to do anything that an individual can do which is not expressly prohibited by other legislation. This activity can include charging or it can be undertaken for a commercial purpose, and could be aimed at benefiting the authority, the area or its local communities. By giving councils the flexibility to act in their own financial interests, the GPC will allow councils to do more than was previously sanctioned under wellbeing powers.

Trading and charging for services has been a feature of local government for a considerable time. For example:

- Specific powers to charge for services are contained in a variety of local government statutes.

- Under the Local Authorities (Goods and Services) Act 1970 councils were given powers to enter into agreements with each other and with a long list of other designated public bodies.

- The Local Government Act 2003 added further possibilities. It enables councils to trade in activities related to their functions on a commercial basis with a view to profit through a company. In addition, the 2003 Act empowers councils to charge for any discretionary services on a cost recovery basis. Originally, trading through a company was confined to certain categories of councils but a Trading Order, in force since October

2009, removed such restrictions.

- The GPC sits alongside local government's existing powers to trade and charge. Under the Localism Act 2011 commercial trading through a special purpose trading company is an option open to many more public bodies including eligible parish councils, fire and rescue authorities, integrated transport authorities, passenger transport executives and economic prosperity boards in England. Powers contained in the Localism Act also provide the ability to charge for discretionary services on a cost recovery basis.

There are specific powers to charge for services scattered throughout local government legislation. For example:

- section 19 of the Local Government (Miscellaneous Provisions) Act 1976 permits charging for the use of leisure and recreational facilities.

- section 38 of the 1976 Act permits entering into agreements with other persons to make full use of local authority computers and equipment.

- the Civic Restaurants Act 1947 permits district councils and London boroughs to run restaurants and otherwise provide for the supply to the public of meals and refreshments and use best endeavours to ensure its income is sufficient to cover its expenditure.

The Local Government Act 2003 introduced a general power to charge for the provision of any discretionary service. The charging power is available to all 'best value authorities'. This includes all counties, unitary authorities, London boroughs, metropolitan boroughs, and districts councils alongside a number of other local authorities.

The charging powers do not apply to services which an authority is mandated or has a duty to provide. However, councils can charge for discretionary services (that is, services they have power to provide but are not obliged or have a duty to provide by law).

The recipient of the discretionary service must have agreed to pay for the provision of such services.

The 2003 Act power cannot be used where charging is prohibited or where another specific charging regime applies. Charging is limited to cost recovery and statutory guidance published in 2003 outlines how costs and charges should be established and that guidance remains in force.

The charging provisions contained in the Localism Act 2011 follow, very closely, the requirements of the 2003 Act to allow local authorities to charge up to full cost recovery for discretionary services. These provisions continue side-by-side rather than replace the Local Government Act 2003 powers. The general power to charge is subject to a duty to secure that, taking one financial year with another, the income from charges does not exceed the costs of provision.

As with the 2003 Act powers, charging for things done in exercise of the GPC is not a power to make a profit from those activities. So authorities wishing to engage in commercial trading for profit will need to rely on other powers to trade.

TRADING

The legislation relevant to local authority trading uses the term 'commercial purpose' to describe trading activities. Government guidance suggests 'commercial purpose' means having a primary objective to make a profit from the trading activities in question. We will use the term 'trading' in a broad way to cover a range of arrangements that councils might wish to enter into to make efficiencies through reducing costs; improving services for the benefit of users and, potentially, to generate profits. These may involve establishing new business relationships with other councils and public bodies or with the private sector, voluntary and community sector and individuals.

For councils considering a new trading venture it will be essential to first determine whether it is acting pursuant to a 'commercial purpose'. If so, the law requires councils to pursue that commercial purpose via a company. If not, alternative arrangements to establishing a company are also explored below.

TRADING WITHIN THE PUBLIC SECTOR

The term 'shared services' in this guide means the provision of services from one public body to one or more others. The very important distinguishing feature of shared service arrangements is that such an enterprise will usually be exclusively comprised of public bodies who will not be seeking to sell services or goods to the general public or to any other party such as a private sector entity. In this way the market is contained, easily identified and limited in range and potential risk. The partners to such an arrangement will all be likely to be sharing the risk and rewards of the venture.

Shared service arrangements can be achieved either:

1. directly through a lead authority and joint committee arrangement, and/or

2. by agreement or contract, or

3. via a delivery vehicle such as a company.

1. The Local Government Act 1972, Section 101 permits local authorities to arrange for the discharge of their functions by a

committee, sub-committee, an officer or by another local authority. Many shared service arrangements are set up under these public administrative arrangements, usually with one of the authorities involved taking the lead.

2. The Local Authorities (Goods and Services) Act 1970 remains the bedrock for establishing shared service or joint arrangements between two or more public bodies through an agreement or contract. It permits councils to enter into 'agreements' with other local authorities or other designated public bodies, for the provision of goods, materials and administrative, professional and technical services, for the use of vehicles, plant and apparatus and associated staff, and for the carrying out of maintenance. These powers remain particularly useful where authorities are seeking to provide goods or services of a relatively modest value to each other, and the costs and time associated with setting up a commercial trading company would be disproportionate.

The 1970 Act leaves it to the public bodies concerned to use an 'agreement' to set out payment terms or otherwise that the parties consider appropriate. This offers flexibility and does not limit arrangements to simply cost recovery. Some councils have established shared services enterprises through a combination of public administrative arrangement such as a joint committee under section 101 of the Local Government Act 1972 and an agreement using 1970 Act powers.

Local authorities (and indeed other public bodies) can use these powers to 'test the waters' and explore whether collaborative arrangements can be established which make for more effective and efficient working.

Tax and fiscal considerations will also be paramount here, as setting up a company creates a new statutory body which may (depending on the type of company established and the trading activities it carries out) be subject to the corporation tax regime and will be treated separately for VAT, National Non-Domestic Rates (NNDR) and stamp duty land tax purposes.

Using an agreement or joint committee structure where the arrangements are established for the better performance of public administration may also provide a better fit with the limited exceptions from EU procurement rules, known as the Teckal exemption, which is briefly outlined below (along with a note about any relevant post Brexit changes). Overall this approach provides time for joint enterprises in the public sector to evolve through a joint committee arrangement and/or by agreement whilst retaining the option to establish a company structure at some later date, if desired.

TECKAL EXEMPTION

Teckal exemption means where an authority or authorities set up arrangements, including wholly owned companies to supply services back to those authorities, in the same manner as an in-house arrangement. In these cases the procurement rules do not apply to those arrangements.

Setting up a company is another route by which public bodies can establish shared services arrangements. Public bodies could, for example, establish a company to perform a trading function of a specific and limited nature to provide services to its member/owners. 'Teckal' compliance features would need to be built into the constitution of the company to ensure its operations and management remain in the control of the owner/members and that the company supplies the significant proportion of its business to those owner/members.

This type of 'Teckal' company would not be expected (or permitted) to trade commercially with the public at large. Local authorities creating a Teckal company need to very clearly articulate what sort of enterprise they are intending to establish and what sort of custom or 'trade' that company would undertake to distinguish it from a more market orientated commercial trading undertaking.

Commercial trading companies, unlike companies set up for trading by and between local authority members would be outward facing and would seek to attract business from any source.

The GPC powers might be used to establish a company which is set up for non-commercial public administrative functions and which is to be wholly under the control of its member local authorities/public bodies. The members should be able to engage with the company without going through a procurement exercise, provided these arrangements are akin to 'in-house' arrangements to comply with the 'Teckal' exemption.

TRADING BEYOND THE PUBLIC SECTOR

After many years of experience trading between public bodies, the Local Government Act 2003 added new possibilities for councils to extend their trading activities to provide services to other users beyond the 'defined public bodies' listed in the 1970 Act. This includes the wider market, private individuals and other bodies or organisations. In 2009 the Government permitted all best value authorities in England "to do for a commercial purpose" anything which they are authorised to do for the purpose of carrying on their ordinary functions.

The Localism Act 2011 has extended opportunities to trade for a commercial purpose much further. For example the General Power of Competence (GPC) does not require councils to identify a statutory function upon which to 'hang' their trading activity. In other words, local authorities are allowed to expand their trading activities into areas not related to their existing functions. It also effectively removes geographical boundaries to local authority activity so that they can set up trading company that can trade anywhere in the UK or elsewhere. But the law continues to prevent councils trading with individuals where they have a statutory duty to provide that service to them already.

GPC also extends trading powers to 'eligible parish councils'. These are defined by the Secretary of State in secondary legislation as parish councils who have:

- two-thirds or more of members of the council who have been elected at ordinary elections or at a by-election, as opposed to being co-opted or appointed,

- a clerk to the parish council who holds one of the listed qualifications and has completed relevant training in the exercise of the GPC, provided in accordance with the National Association of Local Council's national training strategy, and

- passed a resolution that it meets the other conditions of eligibility.

Under both the Local Government Act 2003 and Localism Act 2011, the power to trade must be exercised through a company. There are different definitions of 'company' in the relevant legislation but there appears to be no substantive difference between the types of entity permitted as trading companies, namely companies limited by shares, companies limited by guarantee or industrial and provident societies.

With trading companies wholly owned by a council, any profits generated may go back to the council through dividends or service charges. These can then be used to hold down council tax and/or can be invested into frontline services.

Local authorities may also consider participating in someone else's trading venture through a company, such as a social enterprise, as long as that entity is a company within the relevant definitions. A limited partnership or limited liability partnerships do not fall within the permitted categories for local authority commercial trading.

COMMERCIAL TRADING AND RISK

All commercial activity involves risk and potential losses as well as the potential to make profits. These risks and opportunities must be fully understood and scoped before embarking upon such enterprises, with the potential to mitigate and manage these risks explored. A key part of this is the development of a business case. The 2009 Trading Order requires that a business case ('a comprehensive statement') be prepared and approved before exercising the trading powers. This covers objectives and associated investment and other resources required, business risks with an indication of their significance, and the expected financial results and any other relevant outcomes expected. It also places an obligation on the authority concerned to recover the costs of any accommodation, goods, services, staff or any other thing that it supplies to a company in pursuance of any agreement or arrangement to facilitate the exercise of the trading power.

No similar requirement is currently contained in the Localism Act. In any event the rules on State Aid would need to be considered in this respect. Other important legal, commercial and financial considerations for councils setting up a trading company include company law issues, the cost of bidding for contracts, tax liability (corporation tax and VAT), EU procurement law (at the time of writing this is the case but must be review in the light of Brexit) and state aid rules and employment law (TUPE and pensions). There also needs to be a business plan for the operation of the company.

INTERNAL STRUCTURES

If the aim is full cost recovery then internal structures can be easier to develop than new company models. One model of this that I have seen successfully implemented is that of a Commercial Enterprise Board. The idea behind this is that commercial areas are given special treatment within existing Council governance structures. The board usually consists of senior level members and executive officers. The key commercial areas are 'put' into these boards and report to these boards to maintain strong governance of them. Commercial initiatives operating within these boundaries are allowed to work with slightly reduced financial regulations, procurement regulations, HR etc. They still operate to the legal standard required, but with more flexibility and a lighter touch than the standard council regulations. This gives them the freedom and autonomy to develop new commercial ways of working that respond in a more time effective manner to the requirements of the market.

Changes to the legislative and regulatory environment due to Brexit

The UK's departure from the European Union, (otherwise known as 'Brexit') means that changes to the legislative and regulatory environment within which local authority trading enterprises exist may impact in the longer term. However, until such time as new legislation is enacted and which departs from the processes described in this book, the existing content will remain valid and relevant (e.g. references to Teckal for example). However, the following significant changes have already occurred and should be noted:

Changes to Procurement

Since 1st January 2021 (the end of the Brexit transition

period), the Public Contracts Regulations 2015 (the "PCR") have been amended by the Public Procurement (Amendment etc.) (EU Exit) Regulations 2020 ("the Exit Regulations"). However, the amendments introduced by the Exit Regulations do not change the analysis of the PCR in this publication (e.g as they impact on the so called 'Teckal' exemption). Whilst the changes made by the Exit Regulations to the public procurement regime are limited, in December 2020 the UK Government published a Green Paper on the transformation of procurement, and commenced public consultations, with a view to making substantive changes to the rules, including the PCR.

Changes to State Aid

From 1 January 2021, the EU State aid rules no longer apply to funding and other forms of support measures granted to business by UK public authorities. In place of the EU State aid rules, new provisions are set out in Chapter 3 of Title XI of the new Trade and Cooperation Agreement (the 'TCA'). While the TCA adopts a familiar set of principles to previous EU State aid regulations, the terminology and structure of the rules the UK must adhere is very different. In particular, the concept of 'subsidy' replaces 'State aid' - a recognition that the UK is no longer in the EU Single Market. However, 'Subsidy' is defined in terms which are very similar to the concept of 'aid', meaning that what would have been considered 'aid' before 31 December 2020 is likely to be captured under the Subsidy Control regime from 1 January 2021.

These are issues which need to be kept under review as the procurement and subsidy regime develop in the UK. For further help and information on the implications of Brexit see https://www.localgovernmentlawyer.co.uk/sharpeedge/

15.

BUSINESS DEVELOPMENT

The internal processes required to operate commercially, or rather to have success in operating commercially, often present the biggest change for public sector organisations as they commercialise. Have a look at the Business Development Maturity Matrix below. The headings suggest some of the key areas of process that are required for effective business development. Score your own organisation against these areas between 1 and 3 and see how you come out.

No / Never	**1**
Not Consistently	**2**
Yes Consistently	**3**

We use a specific business development methodology

I have good visibility of the sales pipeline

A Board member is involved in our biggest opportunities

I have regular meetings with colleagues to discuss accounts and opportunities

We use; account opportunity and meeting plans

I can access sales information from a known location on the shared drive

We work with other departments to identify cross-departmental opportunities

We liaise with other divisions to share best practice

The language used in this matrix is quite foreign to most public sector staff. Cut through the language for the moment and can you see the emphasis this places on the customer, their relationship with you and systems to manage that relationship. It is easy to blame your IT systems and their lack of functionality, however massive inroads can be made with free open source software that is readily available or in fact by just using the shared drive on your existing intranet. Tools make it easier, but the most important thing is the mind-set. There is always an improvement that can be made even with existing tools that aren't perfect.

Activity

What new processes do we need to put in place to develop the internal systems needed to succeed commercially?

COMMERCIAL GOV

16.

COVID RECOVERY

I'm finishing this second edition with a chapter specifically about Covid recovery. The pandemic has had a large impact on commercial activity and bottom line finances more generally. Before this pandemic commercial development in local authorities was an increasingly important part of the adaptation and change of councils to operate effectively in the financial, political and social context in which they exist. Covid-19 has exacerbated the drivers for this change and adaptation with the financial imperative to make and/or save greater than it ever has been, whilst demand and need for services is also increasing. In short, financial self-sufficiency, or as close to it as possible given the nature of the council and the service it has a duty to provide, is the goal and commercial development is an increasingly important part of achieving this.

Can we wait for post-covid?

History teaches us that businesses that thrive after tumultuous market conditions are in fact those that adapted best during the crisis. This can be seen in modern history looking back to the great depression of the 1930s, the second world war and more recently, the banking crisis. Businesses that worked hard, understood the environment they were in, how that impacted on their market and adapted during the crisis were far more successful than those who waited for the crisis to be over before responding to it.

The same will be true in this pandemic. Businesses that adapt and respond during this crisis will be the ones that do best afterwards. By continually adapting, the business is in fact ensuring it is in alignment with market needs, whatever those needs are and however they change. This means as the needs change again as we move from the pandemic into recovery, those businesses will already know how the market is responding and will be relevant to emerging needs. Business that don't adapt during the pandemic will be playing catch up in a fast-moving recovery environment and run the risk of never regaining their market relevance.

The same is true for public sector commercial activity. If organisations wait until the pandemic is over before refocusing and adapting their commercial approach they run a high risk of 'missing the market' and being locked into a cycle of trying to catch up – a cycle that drains cashflow rather than generates the income that is so needed.

The challenge is perhaps greater for the public sector as their workload has increased enormously during the pandemic as part of the public sector's emergency response. However, we see a big divide between organisations – those that are 'parking' commercial development until after the crisis is over and those who see commercial development as even more important now and are doing what they can to re position themselves to be commercially relevant in this season and ready for success in the next.

If waiting until we move into a post-covid world means reduced commercial performance not just now, but for the next three to five years, can the public sector afford to do that?

Resetting and refocusing

This season provides an opportunity to do something really important – review our existing commercial activities to determine whether they should continue. Sometimes the most commercial decision is the decision to stop something. Many activities have been labelled under the 'commercial' badge, but are they really operating commercially, and do they really have commercial potential? What didn't work and wasn't commercial before this pandemic, definitely won't be in the new markets we are moving into.

This season, before we fully move into recovery mode, is the ideal time to 'reset' existing commercial activity. To relook at them and ensure there is a clear purpose and vision to the activity, ensure it contributes to corporate objectives and be sure it is properly operating commercially.

It is also the ideal opportunity to refocus our commercial portfolios. Resources are tight and getting tighter so are our commercial activities delivering the return we require and could we gain a better return by focusing resources away from some activities and into others that are performing better and have greater potential?

Most public sector assets and commercial strategies are based on improving the return on assets we hold because "we've always had them" or "we've always done it that way" - now is the time to challenge that thinking.... With some key questions:

- Why do we hold this asset (i.e. is it the best use of the capital and revenue locked up in it)

- Does this traded service really make a commercially acceptable yield for the risk we are taking, or is it merely covering direct costs + a bit (or putting off an unpleasant decision)

- Is the way in which we are providing this service (or meeting a need) really the best way to do it, or could it be better delivered in partnership or via the community?

- Is our commercial strategy actually maximising value against our objectives (social as well financial)

- Is it lopsided rather than meeting a balanced bottom line.

Now, as we are setting our budgets for 2021/22 in an extremely volatile environment, is the time to be challenging ourselves, reviewing what we're doing and developing short, medium and long term plans that see us directing resource and effort that yields the greatest return (social and financial) and removes it from low return ventures.

Understanding the new markets

Understanding the markets in which we are operating is typically something public sector organisations struggle with. In fact, I've seen many business cases and business case templates that pay no account to the markets. However, it is the market that provides the context for the commercial activity and many markets have drastically changed as a result of covid. It is important to ask some questions of the market: has it changed? How has it changed? Is the change permanent or is it temporary? The answers to these questions determines the action that needs to be taken to ensure our commercial activity is in alignment to where the market need and demand is.

Whatever changes to the market there are the following metrics will continue to provide the foundational basis for financial forecasts:

- How many potential customers are there?

- What is their typical or average spend?

- What percentage of the market is realistic for us to occupy?

Collaboration and Innovation

The financial challenges are large, and we can't expect to solve them using the same thinking and actions we used before. We need new, innovative solutions and we need to work on a bigger scale to solve bigger problems. Innovation rarely happens by accident. If it does it is a one off, a fluke. The most innovative companies have a specified innovation strategy and innovation process. The same is needed for local authorities. The number of organisations we work with who are disappointed because 'staff haven't generated good ideas' is high. What is worse than this though, is that staff then become demoralised when nothing is done with the ideas they have put forward. This becomes a vicious circle that ends in disengagement in the commercial challenge.

We need to embrace innovation and drive it with a clear and thought through process such as the step suggested by Turner in his excellent book 'Be Less Zombie':

1. Identify the right opportunities

2. Design innovating questions

3. Generate ideas

4.   Assessing and selecting ideas

5.   Testing assumptions with experiments

6.   Scaling and integrating experiments

7.   Identifying viable business models

We also need to collaborate to identify economies of scale made possible by working together as well as new ways of inspiring each other to think and act differently. This is something we are trying to work towards by setting up the *£Billion Challenge* – https://billionchallenge.co.uk

Diversifying our portfolios

This pandemic has shown many public sector commercial portfolios to be unintentionally narrow. By commercial portfolio I don't just mean property portfolio, although exactly the same applies to our commercial property portfolios. We need to diversify the range of commercial opportunities we are exploring to minimise the risk and extend our opportunity for success in many differing market conditions.

Part of diversifying our commercial portfolio is perhaps down to diversifying our definition of what 'commercial' means. For many it is limited to commercial property or maybe income generation. Both will continue to be important parts of the commercial mix for local authorities. However, there are many other aspect of 'being commercial' that we can grasp and in so doing, will help us to diversify our commercial portfolios, reduce risk and in the process find new opportunities that improve our bottom line. Some other 'commercial' activities that have the potential to drive bottom line results are:

Market moderation or management – using the purchasing power and influence of the local authority and other commercial entities the authority may have to drive up quality and reduce price in the local market

Demand management – front loading systems and working with early intervention services to reduce demand for intensive and expensive services

Contract management – improve our negotiation and contract management skills so we get better deals and better performance from our contracts

Place shaping – embedding commercial development in our economic development. Making local authority infrastructure central to new development and developing our local areas so they are attractive for businesses to locate in the area. This drives up the prosperity of our communities and will lead to increased business rate receipts.

Culture

Finally, we have an opportunity to reset the culture of our organisations. The window for this is narrowing as we all become used to new ways of working. In the early stages of the pandemic, everything was thrown in the air and public sector performance levels were incredible as staff worked in new ways to provide new services and emergency response.

We have an opportunity to identify the culture change that the emergency brought about, the drivers for that change and further important elements of a future commercial culture. Now is the time to set these as our ongoing culture so all decisions across our services are made in a business-like manner.

Culture is the environment in which our strategies grow. We need to know what environment is needed for our commercial strategies to reach their potential and work hard to create that environment across our organisations.

About the Author

David Elverson is the Managing Director of Commercial Gov, a specialist consultancy he set up in 2016. Before this David has been involved in supporitng commercial development across the public sector since 2001. Commercial Gov operates across the Public Sector working extensively with local authorities, central government, the NHS, the MOD and many other public bodies. They also work with governments from other countries supporting their commercial ambitions.

Commercial Gov has expertise across a wide definition of 'commercial': income generation, asset utilisation, market management, innovation and cost reduction.

They provide insight, challenge and development to support sustainable commercial development. They help you to develop the capabilities needed to manage your own commercial growth.

For more information visit:

www.commercialgov.co.uk

or email

info@commercialgov.co.uk

CPSIA information can be obtained
at www.ICGtesting.com
Printed in the USA
BVHW040546060421
604308BV00014B/1099